WHO W BRIN RAMRAJYA

of My Dream and
How It Can Be Achieved

AMIT SHARMA

PRABHAT
PAPERBACKS

Published by
PRABHAT PAPERBACKS
An imprint of Prabhat Prakashan Pvt. Ltd.
4/19 Asaf Ali Road,
New Delhi-110 002 (INDIA)
e-mail: prabhatbooks@gmail.com

ISBN 978-93-5521-752-3
WHO WILL BRING RAMRAJYA
by Amit Sharma

© Reserved

Edition
First, 2023

Price

Printed at

Foreword

*I*n 2013, when I started taking an interest in India politics, I was aware of the circumstances of the country since I was in Class 10th. But, I felt so helpless, when a new government came to power in 2014. I was hopeful for the country but soon I realised that there is a nexus of negative elements in the country that don't want solutions to happen. I found that the people of the country had made up their mind that corruption can never end, irrespective of the government is in power. Then I decided to find solutions of problems of the country and now explaining you them in detail. I reached these solutions after so many revisions in the first idea and in the last part of the book I am telling how to finance these suggestions. Solutions are easy and don't demand so many changes to be made in the constitution, and if a leader is well intentioned he can implement them easily. Even though these suggestions do not get implemented, I want more people to read this book so that they could discuss these suggestions and understand that the solutions of the nation's problems are not impossible to realise.

Contents

6

❑

1 Ramrajya of My Dream

1. Politics must be clean and must be free from crime and corruption. Leaders must be among the best human beings in terms of mind and heart. There must be a system that if a leader becomes a liability for the nation due to his negligence, ego or ill will then he can be held accountable and punished as a normal citizen.

2. There must be a universal public healthcare system capable to serve the whole population of the country either free or at the lowest cost. Treatment of every disease must be available for every citizen at a public hospital at the lowest cost. There must be no death in the country due to lack of funds for treatment of any illness/disease of any citizen.

3. There must be income security for everyone in the nation as per the value created by him either in terms of labour/production/intellectual property rights. All farmers must have assurance that after harvesting there will be a guarantee of a certain price for a specific quality. Also, the farmers must be assured that their entire produce will be purchased either by a private player or the government. If the harvest of a farmer gets destroyed by a natural calamity then he must be compensated fully.

4. There must be an impartial, quick and qualitative delivery of justice to every citizen without considering the economic, social or political status or connection of any citizen.

5. There must be a proper system in the whole country so that the police could perform its duties impartially and their image in the general population stays honourable.

6. Education is a public service and any public service must be qualitative, accessible, efficient, and affordable. In present affordable education means public education which in most or many parts of the country is not qualitative. The education which is qualitative, it is not affordable in most or many parts of the country. So there must be a universal common minimum curriculum for the primary, secondary and higher education throughout the country. Technology the future of every sector of economy and country. Technology has made life comfortable, accessible and affordable and the same applies to the education sector. Experiential learning may add golden value to this effort.

7. The administration in India has become used to its authority and less accountability and this has created a casual attitude. Many civil servants are also doing exceptional work but seeing the complexity of the Indian population and its problems that is very limited and less than enough. In a Ramrajya a civil servant must always feel himself less than the most common citizen of the country, he has to keep this fact in mind. The authority must be only for criminals and wrongdoers. There must be target-oriented work for civil servants.

8. Corruption has become an innate part of politics, administration and even society; unfortunately it has also become one of the motivation factors fo the people to enter politics and public services. The people have acquired so much money by abusing their rights that were given to them for public good which they could have never earned by using their skills, hardwork and intelligence. In fact appointment

of such people has proved detrimental for the public but the same money has become their shield and they know that. Corruption is the main reason of crime and inaction in most of the arenas of government function. In Ramrajya, there will be a minimum level of corruption. A corrupt person will not be regarded in society. Such a system must be created where there will be no way to conceal the corruption money within the country.

9. When there will be less corruption in the country then there will be far more resources available in the hands of people and the government. And by allocating these resources judiciously, most of the population can be covered in employment. In Ramrajya, there will be no crisis of unemployment.

10. There are many faultlines in the society. In Ramrajya, there will be an ideal society.

11. All the efforts to achieve these aims has to be started firstly at the thought level and for that humans need to have progressive thinking and there should be a re-engineering of thought process. A whole part of this book is devoted only for this.

12. Many laws need to be introduced to make Ramrajya a reality and many questions need to be answered for the clarity of thoughts. In Ramrajya, the whole system of the government and administration will review their progress themselves and see the results of public feedback system and will continue their effort to improve their governance and behaviour. There will be an outcome analysis in all sectors of the country of all government efforts every year by an independent agency of civil society. If there is degradation, no improvement or a very minor improvement then the government will change its policies after extensive discussions with stakeholders and it will be done every year. And in future all governments in the country will be allocated KRAs either as per their

manifesto or directly by the public through voting and every year ratings of performance will be given to all governments in the country.

13. In Ramrajya, no girl will work as a bonded sex worker, no child will beg on the streets and instead he/she will study and no senior citizen will be without food, shelter and care. No physically handicapped person will be without artificial organs and even no animal will be without food. ❏

2 Re-engineering Institutional Process

Technology and Innovation Commission

The government will ask the department of personnel and training to provide a list of responsibilities and duties that all civil servants must fulfil at different posts. Then an act will be brought and with this act a vision statement behind bringing this act will be uploaded on the government website. In this act all state governments will be bound by the recommendation of the chief technology and innovation officer of the state. A department will be created under this act and the chief of this department will be appointed by the council of the Prime Minister and Supreme Court Chief Justice.

Under this act, it will be mandatory for every ministry of state the governments and central government to appoint a chief technology and innovation officer in every ministry. All these officers will be temporary or on contract basis and will be given a fixed salary as per the contract. But a goal will be given to every ministry or every department. If the chief technology and innovation officer succeeds in achieving that goal then that certain amount which may be between one crore to ten crore will be given to that officer. In this way the best minds will emerge.

This department will be given the duty to digitalize every process or work of the state and central government.

Government's Information System

A Government's Information System will be created and a Citizen's Information File of every citizen will be created. User ID of citizen will be his/her Aadhar card number. After making every service online in the country, this citizen's information file will have data of earnings, savings in the form of deposits and shares, NSCs, land purchased, sold and owned by citizens as well as total expenditure of citizens in the year. It will also have the record of citizen's health history, police case history, education history and the amount of money they have transferred to their family members. Only the chief minister's office, prime minister's office and tax authorities will have the right to see this citizen's information file. Police authorities can only check the police record of a citizen by his Aadhar number. Tax authorities can have access to their financial data. Health authorities can access their health data but corruption control committee can have access to the entire data of a citizen along with the PMO and CMO. First step required to accomplish this will be to digitize land records and link them with the Aadhar number.

How to Make Land Records and History Online and Link them with the Aadhar Number

Every sub-district tehsildar will have to arrange 300 data entry operators. An ID on the land records portal will be created of these data entry operators. Every data entry operator will be ordered to update 30 records online daily with the GPS location of the land. Ten lakhs data entry operators will update 3 crores land records daily. Tehsildar or sub-registrar will delegate his powers to a hundred officials of many departments and they will authorize these land records with their digital signature. Within some days all land records with their history will be updated throughout the country. There are two questions that arise now.

14

How the Aadhar numbers will be updated?

Answer:-

First way:

1. Lands purchased in the last five years will have Aadhar as a document so there is no need to get Aadhar number and where Aadhar number is not present, the Voter ID Card will be present. All lekhpals will be given the Voter ID photocopy and it will be their duty to go to villages and collect the Aadhar number of such voter card holders.

2. Lands where the owner has died long ago but land has not been transferred to the legal heirs. Such land records will be updated when it gets transferred to the legal heirs.

3. If some state governments don't want to participate in the process then it can be done in all those states that agree.

Second way: India has 150 crores of population out of which around 125 crores have the Aadhar cards. Twenty-five crores of population which don't have Aadhaar are mostly women and children of rural India who don't normally own land and properties. Since hundreds of years or more than that it is a practice that when somebody purchases a land or property then at the time of registry the buyer gives his fingerprints of all fingers. The same as temperature scanner, a hand holding scanner will be invented and attached with the desktops of data entry operators. They will scan the fingerprints and then the site will search for the Aadhar number of the same fingerprints. Then the data entry operator will submit and create a queue. This queue will reach the sub-registrar or officers to whom the sub-registrar will delegate his powers. On the desktop screen of officers, name, photo, father's name and address of land owner and the Aadhar card holder will be displayed and he will match the data and authorize the list.

Thus within 15 days, the Aadhaar numbers will get updated in all the land records. As the queue gets authorized, a message on the phone number registered on Aadhar will be sent automatically and a letter with all the details will be dispatched to the Aadhaar card owners.

All landowners will have to go to common service centres and login with the credentials given in the letter and will give their fingerprints. If again these fingerprint matches with the scanned fingerprints in the registry then their Aadhar will get linked with the property. After this process, three months notice period or waiting period will be given to the entire population. If anybody wants to register their claim on the land or property then they can present it within three months to the sub-registrar. Details of all lands and properties will be shown on the government website. If they fail or their claim is rejected or nobody registers their claim then a copy of the title deed will be sent to the Aadhar card owner.

As these land records will be online by the Aadhar number then the Registered Mortgage Act and SARFAESI Act will be abolished and a new act will be made under which a banker after sanctioning a loan with the thumb impression of the owner can create the queue for registration of mortgage and when this queue is authorized by the sub-registrar, then the enforceable land mortgage will be created in favour of the bank.

There will be no need for banks to get title investigation report by lawyers as all data related to land records and history will be available for bankers by just entering the Aadhar numbers. They will have a printout of the land record and its history and they will keep it with the Loan Documents.

The Aadhar card has been fed into 80 per cent of accounts so the government will create a system under RBI that all accounts linked with one Aadhar and one Udyog Aadhar will show in the citizen's information file of the citizen and all transactions in these accounts will reflect on the Government Information System site.

The police records will be linked with Aadhar.

Health information will be linked with Aadhar.

Educational degrees and progress will also be linked with Aadhar.

All government services will be linked with Aadhar.

All expenditure above ₹ 5,000 will also be linked with Aadhar.

Aadhar ATM will be issued to all citizens and if they use any service or purchase anything above ₹ 5,000 then they will just have to show ATM on the POS machine and Aadhar will get captured.

Every department such as the judiciary, police and universities will be provided IDs, passwords and funds to update all records of cases, educational backgrounds, and professional backgrounds for those who have any kind of professional licenses by the government or its institutes. Police after registering an FIR will have to submit the enquiry report and charge sheet online to the court with the authorization of the digital signature of the authorized official.

Public Information System

Every citizen of India will be provided an email ID either on gmail or on nic.in. Email ID will be based on their Aadhar number like if your aadhar number is 124578963214 then your email ID will be 124578963214@gmail.com or nic.in. The ID and password will be sent on the mobile number registered on Aadhar. A citizen can change the password through OTP authentication on the mobile number registered in Aadhar number. Citizens who change their password successfully; email IDs of such citizens will be sent to banks to update in their account link with the same Aadhar, if these accounts don't already have any email ID.

If a citizen applies for any government service then the government official will ask for the Aadhar number and all progress of government service and resolution will be sent on his Aadhar email ID. If the government wants to send its plans and progress, then it will send them to these email IDs.

One crore party activists will get involved and will be instructed to make a whatsapp group of 25 members (one from each family) of that area, thus covering the whole population. One hundred such activists will form a group and all officials like SHO, SDM, MLA and MP will be a part of this group.

One group will be made in every state where all MLAs, DMs, SSPs, all secretaries, chief ministers and prime minister will be a part of this group.

One group of all chief ministers, chief of all PSUs, industry body, all senior officials of central government with the prime minister will be made.

In this way, the prime minister can reach to every citizen of India within a minute and if any citizen of India faces problems then he can also reach to prime minister or chief minister.

Public Feedback System

An android app will be made where citizens can login with their Aadhar based email id and can give their feedback for the services provided to them in the last six months and can also suggest any improvements needed. This feedback will go to an employee and his reporting authority. After every six months reports of all employees of the state government department, PSUs, and central government department will be sent to the chief minister and prime minister. I know that the whole population can't give feedback but many will agree to do so.

Citizen Suggestion Portal

A citizen suggestion portal will be created where any citizen can login with their Aadhar based email ID and can give suggestions for the betterment of the nation and governance. Suggestions which will be accepted by the government will be awarded monetarily and prestigiously.

Economic Census

An economic census will be done by the central government. When the Citizen Information File is created then the economic status in the form of grade from A to E will be given to every citizen considering their deposits in banks, land holding and expenditure in the last twelve months. And all the service charges and taxes will be decided as per the economic status of the citizen.

Equality Commission

This commission will be formed to analyse the inequality level in the nation and will keep suggesting that the government should make such policies which will increase equality and bridge the gap between the rich and poor. The commission will be a permanent commission and will give ratings to all the states in terms of equality every year.

Social Justice Commission

This commission will gather data and submit its report with suggestions to the central government and all state government on the social justice index. All states will be rated by this commission every year in terms of social justice in the state in the previous year. This will also be a permanent commission.

Central Medical Commission

This commission will be an administrative body for all health services, whether public or private in the country. This commission will open its branches in every commissionary of the country and if anybody wants to have a medical certificate for absence from a criminal case hearing then they will have to get their medical certificate certified by the central medical commissioner's office. This office will also send a doctor to the residence of the patient.

Corruption Control Committee

A legal body will be formed named the Corruption Control Committee. This body will be constituted with 50 members of civil society and 50 members of the judiciary, central government and all state governments. The 50 members of civil society will be selected by online voting and their tenure will last for 3 years and they will be allowed to contest again. They will be paid adequately for their services.

Corruption Intelligence Unit

A Corruption Intelligence Unit will be formed and initially there will be a recruitment of 10,000 officers. They will be selected after a hard and thorough process. Five officers will be sent to every district of the country and they will provide information about corruption in those districts. Then every corruption case will be given to an investigation officer. He will investigate and collect proofs, and then submit the report to the Corruption Control Committee. The committee will issue warrants and the corrupt people will get arrested. These officers will get interchanged between districts and states. This unit will report to the Corruption Control Committee.

Revenue Intelligence Unit

Similar to the Corruption Intelligence Unit, a Revenue Intelligence Unit will be formed. Initially 10,000 officers will be recruited and 5 officers will be sent to every district. They will provide tax theft information to the unit's head office. Then this unit will collect proof or raid those people and recover the due taxes. This unit will report to the Corruption Control Committee.

Implementation and Monitoring Council

This council will be formed to monitor the implementation of all plans and schemes of the central government and state governments. The council will have 50 members of civil society and 50 members of the judiciary, central government, state governments and media. At half-yearly intervals, the council will publish its observations on how much time has been taken in implementation of each policy and will rate the state governments and central government in terms of implementation speed.

❏

3 Re-engineering Political Process

At present, politics is very unproductive and we can even say counter-productive for the Indian society because politics has become a game of money and power. Here anybody who does not have crores of rupees with power cannot think of fighting and winning elections. Political parties spend thousands of crores over elections of the states and these elections happen every five years.

This money is taken from mafias, criminals, businessmen and industrialists. Later politicians are bound to benefit and protect these people from the consequences of their wrong doings.

Those seated on any higher chair know it. The limit of expenditure the Election Commission decides for an MLA Election candidate is being spent by a village pradhan in elections. Politics says that it will eradicate poverty of citizens but it has become a poverty eradication programme for politicians. People want to have decent people in politics but like to vote for disreputable people in elections. If a politician thinks of eradicating corruption then he feels he is alone and weak to do so. He thinks, if he puts these mafias of every district in jail then who would fund them in the next elections? These mafias may arrange money collectively and bribe corrupt MLAs and MPs and these corrupt MLAs or MPs will either switch parties or resign from their post and the chief minister or prime minister may have to resign from his post. In India money has become the first God, many MLAs and MPs are not loyal to the country and their party. They are first loyal to money and their positions. People are not educated or I can say not well educated. When a politician comes in his cars with twenty bodyguards, people applaud him while when an honest person arrives in his single car for canvassing, people don't come to listen to him. So, people have also become glamorized.

Public Funding of Elections

Firstly, we need to understand that reforming is a continuous process. First reform in politics is public funding of elections. Election Commission had called a meeting of all political parties for taking their views for public funding of elections. Most of the regional parties agreed but some national parties did not agree, do you know why?

Because these political parties spend hundreds of crores or more than that on public rallies, elections advertisements and many other things. The Election Commission can fund only the expenditure of the candidate so these parties refused the proposal.

Reforming is always painful for the people who has lost something because of it but if it is beneficial for the whole population then the country needs to ignore their pain.

The first thing to do is that Election Commission must increase the expenditure limits of MLA's and MPs elections. MLA election expenditure limit should be up to ₹ 2 crores and for MPs election, the candidate should be allowed to spend up to ₹ 5 crores.

The Election Commission can present a proposal in front of the media and the general public. All political parties and every candidate of any national or state level party can get ₹ 2 crores in the state election if that party has more than 5 MLAs in the state's legislation assembly. For MPs election, every national or state level party candidate will get ₹ 5 crores for fighting elections and the same rule of 5 MLAs apply to it. If a party does not have 5 MLAs in the state legislature and wants to contest elections then it will have to contest at his own expenses.

If that party does not win any seat but succeeds in getting more then 5 to 10 per cent votes cast the then election expenditure up to the above mentioned limits will be reimbursed to candidates of these parties by the Election Commission.

If any independent candidate contests election and succeeds in winning, then the Election Commission will reimburse the expenditure up to the above mentioned limits on the production of expenditure receipts.

All the national parties as well as state level parties will be allowed to accept donations but not a single rupee in cash. Every donation whether that is of ₹ 1 or ₹ 1,000 crores, it should be online transfer and website of these parties will have to show the name of the person donating the amount. All political parties will not be allowed to take donations from one account and same person for more than 5 times a year. Electoral bonds scheme will be dismantled.

India has around 5,000 MLAs. In a single state there are estimated not more than 5 political parties which have more than 5 MLAs. So, the total expenditure of public funding of the state elections will be 5,000 × 5 × 2 = 50,000 crores in five years and for MPs elections it will be 545 x 5 x 5 = 15,000 crores. So, total expenditure will be 65,000 crores for five years. This means 13,000 crores per year and it can be gained by increasing one rupee on petrol, diesel or by imposing an election cess.

Debarment from Contesting Elections on Resignation or Swithching the Party

A law amendment should be made. If an MLA or MP during his tenure switches his political party, then he would be debarred from contesting elections for ten years. His membership will be cancelled up to five years. Since he is switching the party, he will also not be able to hold any government post or contract. If an MLA or MP resigns during his tenure then he would not be allowed to contest elections for five years.

CAG Audit of Accounts of All Lawmakers

The third reform is that accounts of every public representative from gram pradhan to Member of Parliament or member of legislative assembly with their family members will be monitored and audited by CAG. A monthly report will be sent by CAG to the Prime Minister and all chief ministers. It may help in curbing irregular practices. If this is successful, then it will also be implemented for all government servants. Enough recruitment can be made in CAG department for this.

Parliament to Open 365 Days

Parliament and all legislative assemblies must be open for 365 days a year except on the public holidays. Twenty-five per cent attendance must be made mandatory for lawmakers. It will close the ordinance route for the government and will help to increase democracy in the country. If any issue is persistent in the country, then the lawmakers will not have to wait for parliament or the legislative assembly to open to raise the issue.

Releasing of Election Manifesto on the Same Time and Date

Election Commission must issue a directive that all political parties contesting in the election will be needed to release the election manifesto or vision statement exactly one month before the polling of the first phase at a fixed time for all political parties.

The nation will wait for ten years after implementing these reforms. It will see what positive change has emerged, what changes are still needed and what are the loopholes; and it will create policy as per requirement after ten years.

In future a law will be made mandatory for every political party to select ten candidates in every constituency and ask voters whom they want to be contested from their seat. Profile of ten candidates will be shown to people, where their history, integrity, criminal records, assets, business, family and everything will be told to the voters. Voters will decide which party should give the ticket to which candidate.

Once India is educated enough, then a law will be made where a written test and psychological test will be put in place for fighting elections and people who will clear this tough test will be able to select from which party they want to contest and they will be funded for election. Even if they lose, they will be given lifetime pension benefit. All these candidates who pass the written test will be called for training for the psychological test for ten days and in these ten days, every activity and discussion they do in their room or on their phone will be monitored by the central team and then it will be decided whether they should be selected or not.

❑

Digital Primary Healthcare

The government will create an android app wherein all the data of all the books, journals and experiences of thousands of physicians and specialist doctors will be fed in the database of this app. When an individual login to the app, he has to select his symptoms, then the robo in the app will either suggest a pathological test or will ask further questions and then it will prescribe the cheapest and effective medicines to the user. After the pathological test a user can easily convert the file of test report into a file compatible to be analysed by the robo. The robo will analyse the file and will ask questions and then it will prescribe medicines. The database will keep updating on a daily basis.

125 AIIMS and 500 Medical Colleges

All the district hospitals will be converted into medical colleges; whether the government has to create a new building for it or it has to expand the existing building. Specialists of every ailment will be appointed depending on the salary the government gives.

In every such medical college, medical seats will be increased up to 1,000 students. In every commissionary, there will be a branch of AIIMS. In every district there will be 100 medically equipped vans with physicians who will operate and each van will be given an area of ten villages.

These vans will go to villages and see the patients. The vans will devote one hour for every village. Every medical college and branch of AIIMS will have an air ambulance for emergency use. An FD of 100 crores for 1,000 branches of AIIMS, medical colleges, etc. will be opened by the central government in the name of the chief medical officer of the district or director of the medical college or AIIMS. The interest will be transferred on monthly basis into the account of the hospital and with this interest, the chief medical officer has to pay for the salary and fuel of medical vans, salary, fuel and maintenance of air ambulance. With the rest of the money he can have maintenance and cleaning of premises. Also if he thinks right, he can purchase any medical equipment for the hospital as per need. Six crores of interest will be enough for that. All the expenditure of interest will be audited by CAG at the end of the year.

The Government Information System will be created and Health Information System will be a part of it. The Health Information System of all the states will be integrated with the Health Information System of the central government. When anybody get any kind of prescription or treatment from any government or private hospital, the prescription test reports and history will be uploaded on the Health Information System website. It will enable all the state governments of the country to know the number of patients of every disease and it will also help in identifying future pandemics.

If possible then the common goal of the country within five or ten years must be set. The central government needs to hold talks with all state governments and make them agree to achieve common goals legally. If India needs to spend 5 lakh crores per year on healthcare as per country's common goal, then the agreed states will need to allocate a certain amount to meet the total allocation target of 5 lakh crores.

If somebody feels that healthcare, education, agricultrue is a state subject and first responsibility to allocate funds is with the state government then I want to say that the central government is earning 40 per cent of total taxes of the country and out of GST share of states is given but share from income tax is not given to any state. The central government has first responsibility to solve the problems of the country.

A rule will be made that manufacturer including manufacturers of medicines will not be allowed to take a profit more than 100 per cent of the production cost.

❑

5 Re-engineering Agriculture Process

Food Bank of India

The government must create a public sector undertaking which may be titled as the Food Bank of India. Then this PSU can apply for project finance of ₹ 6 lakh crores to all public sector banks. The government must provide full guarantee to this finance to PSBs. This PSU will open one branch in every sub-district tehsil. There will be a cold storage of 2 lakh tonnes capacity. One lakh tonnes capacity for cereals and one lakh tonnes capacity for fruits, vegetables and other products. The farmer will go into this branch with his produce and this branch will get it weighed in the godown and then the farmer will get a computerized slip with the details of quality and quantity of his produce and his Aadhar number. The officer in the branch will take the computerized slip and will have his thumb impression and an overdraft account against agri-crops will be opened with the sanctioned amount equivalent to the value of his crop as per current MSP. The officer will debit this account and will transfer the money into the account of the farmer.

An electronic dealer finance account of all kirana, fruits and vegetables shopkeepers or street vendors will be opened. They will go to the Food Bank of India and will collect the produce and the amount will be deducted from their EDFS account by getting a voucher signed by them.

Shopkeepers will be allowed to sell produce at 20 per cent profit and street vendors will be allowed to sell at 30 per cent profit. Everyone will be given licenses by the Food Bank of India and any shopkeeper or street vendor who does not comply with the instructions, their licenses will be cancelled.

This means 10 per cent profit of Food Bank of India. Any produce will not be sold more than the 140 per cent of the MSP of the produce. These shopkeepers and street vendors have to go to the bank and deposit the sale proceeds into their EDFS account.

All shopkeepers and street vendors will have to give a security amount equivalent to their one month sale to the Food Bank of India and within 15 days all dues must be cleared in EDFS A/C. If EDFS account of any shopkeeper or street vendor is inactive due to non-payment then he will not be given any further produce for sale.

Within one year all the overdraft accounts will be closed by sale of produce and Food Bank of India will have a profit of ₹ 3 lakh crores.

The project finance will be of 5 years instead of 20 years and Food Bank will be free of loans within five years and after deducting all expenses like losses on exports and imports (maximum 40,000 crores), and operating cost with wastage(maximum 60,000 crores), EMI (maximum 130,000 crores). From the first year, it will give 70,000 crores profit to the government. MSP will keep on increasing as per the inflation rate in the country.

Nutritional requirement as well as financial requirement of India and Indian Agriculture. An average Indian consumes 68.57 kg wheat per year, 15.71 kg of pulses per year, 77 eggs per year, 3 kg of meat every year, and 70 kg of rice per year. The 30 per cent of the Indian population is vegetarian.

The average Indian consumes 13,620 to 18,900 grams of protein in a year by food consumed where the demand is 23,725 grams of protein every year as the average weight is 65.

Instead of getting 65 grams of protein every day, Indians are consuming 43 grams of protein every day, the remaining needs of protein may be fulfilled by vegetables and fruits. Milk but an average Indian or mainly a poor Indian uses most of the milk for tea that burns its nutritional value. Indians consume more wheat and rice instead of pulses and eggs. We need to double our production of pulses so that the price will be too low and Indians will start consuming it. We need to de-motivate production of meat in the country. We need to have average consumption of pulses of 36 kg per year per person and 300 eggs per person for 70 per cent of the population.

Seeing all this the government needs to formulate a policy after implement of idea of food bank of India that this quantity of this crop or product need to be produced in India and then will make effort to achieve the target. The government will use Gram-panchayat land and will show farmers of every village by producing the required crops in an area of that village.

A list will be made by the government of crops if produced can earn more money for farmers. Food Bank of India will issue a draw and interested farmers from every tehsil will be asked to participate. Farmers who participate will be given interest free KCC as per the scale of finance of that crop. Five officers in every branch of the Food Bank of India will have a duty to daily monitor the progress of crops grown by such farmers. In this way we will be able to get the work done and will be able to increase farmer's income. Soon most of the farmers will move to such crops provided there is enough demand for such produce in the domestic and international market.

Food processing throughout the world can procure only 2 per cent of crops produced as per the demand from all countries of the world but as income will increase this figure can increase. Food processing units can be installed by creating a different PSU in future.

6 Re-engineering Judiciary Process

*I*f an officer does not have enough staff as per the customers inflow, then providing services will be an uphill task. The government will create a Union Judicial Services Commission and will make a provision to recruit lower level to upper level judges through it. The Supreme Court Chief Justice will be the head of this commission and he will decide how many judges and subordinates need to be recruited. Now the country has more than 3 crore cases pending and there are around 17,000 Judges in all courts which means 2,000 cases for each judge.

We need to recruit 50,000 judges so that this ratio can be minimized to 500 cases per judge. The government needs to allocate 100,000 crores for judicial infrastructure throughout the country and this will be the responsibility of the Supreme Court to get the land acquired by the district administration and get the construction done. Then we need to link the judiciary with productivity linked incentive.

If a judge of the district court finalizes a criminal case within one year or six months then he should be rewarded with ₹ 10,000/- per case and same should be if a high court judge finalizes a criminal case within a stipulated time. The judge should be rewarded with ₹ 25,000/- per case for the Supreme Court.

There will be a Corruption Control Committee where the Chief Justice of the Supreme Court, PM and all chief ministers will be part of it. Also the civil society members will be a part of it. If a citizen has any proof of corruption in the judiciary, administration and politics then he will send it on the email ID and fax of this commission, his name will be kept secret and authorities will take action against those corrupt people after investigation. A provision will be made that video and audio recordings of all the hearings of the district court, High court and Supreme Court will be preserved for future analysis.

KRA will be allocated to all judges and a public feedback system will be introduced and judges who settle the most cases within one year and have good reputation as per public feedback system will get promotion. Otherwise, they will not get promotion. Judges who continuously settle cases later than one year will be transferred to the civil court. Also, we need to remove impediments in the way of judiciary to settle cases early.

After enhancing the capacity of the judiciary, no judge will be allowed to give a date later than one month.

No party in a criminal case will be allowed to avoid presence in hearing on medical grounds for more than 3 months. After that they will have to provide a medical certificate verified by the central medical commissioner's office.

The central medical commissioner will open its branches in every commissionary, if any individual takes leave from presence then it will certify it.

Secondly, in every district, and CJM court, there will be a wider conferencing room. If any person of any party in any criminal case can not be present in a court in India on medical grounds or for any other reason, he will go to this court and give his statement on video conferencing.

If judges feel that there is a delay on the part of the police official and they are unable to settle the case within one year and it is destroying their career, then all such judges of India will send the list of such police officials to the Supreme Court. Then Supreme Court will decide and ask them to give their statement as to why they delayed to save themselves from punishment.

As per the economic census, citizens will be given grades from A to E. The grade A will be given to every MP, MLA and people on higher position of all systems. The process will be made online and if anybody wants a public service he has to apply on the government portal.

The Equality Commission will see how fast services are being provided for grade A person to grade E person. It will release data to the public and will make necessary corrections to ensure the same pace of delivery of service for all citizens.

It will also be seen if the accused in a criminal case belongs to the higher grade A and B and for how long his case is pending in the court.

❑

Re-engineering Police Process

An appeal should be filed in the Supreme Court over very slow progress of investigations of criminal cases by police of different states. The Supreme Court may ask all state governments to submit data of criminal cases pending in the country where charge sheets have not been submitted. The Supreme Court will order all state governments to finish investigation within six months in all criminal cases registered till date. Otherwise, the Supreme Court will have to take strict action. If after six months the state governments fail to submit charge sheets in all criminal cases.

The Supreme Court will interpret the Constitution in such a way that investigation is not a state subject as only public order is their subject and will order that there will be a separate police department for investigation at the district level. There will be SSP investigation at the district level and at the state level there will be DGP investigation. All such departments of states will be headed by a committee where 50 per cent of the committee will be civil society members and 50 per cent will be the representative of the Supreme Court, high courts, central government and all state governments. There are huge chances that state governments will not implement this order.

So, the Supreme Court will attach a sentence in its order that if within six months such departments are not created or the order does not get implemented by the state governments, then after six months local police investigation in all criminal cases will not remain legal and will not be accepted by the courts across the country.

The central government will try to pass laws to overturn the order but immediately the Supreme Court will keep striking down such laws. There will be a constitutional chaos and from it, solutions will rise. If the state governments do not wish to give its officers to this department then they will be recruited by the central government. There are around 40,000 average criminal cases pending in the country in every district. Each SSP investigation will be allotted KRA in the form of number of cases they have to finish investigation in that year. Then SSP investigation will allot KRA to all his subordinate officers in the form of cases to be resolved.

❑

8 Re-engineering Education Process

Digital Education is the solution. Many say that it makes a child eyes weak and it is detrimental to his physical and mental health. But, it is not so. There are two ways to implement this and both ways need to be implemented.

First Way-

An interactive app will be created and the entire knowledge of all books of all classes, and of all streams will be updated in the app.

Every chapter, every question and every problem will be given a numeric code and this code will be printed after the question, chapter or problem in NCERT books. If any students or child want to understand any chapter, question or problem, then he will have to enter the code with the problem and robot on this interactive app will give him/her a solution in the app with a video.

Videos on Youtube will also be uploaded. With these codes the student will just need to enter the code in search column of Youtube and he will get the video.

An institution like NCERT will be created for higher studies books. The Books released by this institution will only be eligible for purchase for higher studies courses.

Second Way-

A TV channel will be opened for each class from nursery to Class 12th. Then one TV channel will be opened for every subject. All these channels will be live on Youtube and a video of each session will be uploaded on Youtube. The government will hire professors of IIMs and IITs for subjects of management and technology. Any family that has a TV set can see the channels without spending a single penny for dish connection.

Now, the question arises that what will all the teachers do? If everything gets digital, then a department will be created in every district where all the teachers, professors and principals will sit and attend the calls of students who could not understand something in any online session. A separate TV channel will be set up for teaching different languages. English will be taught between 8:00 pm to 9:00 pm and Hindi will be taught between 9:00 pm to 10:00 pm. All these channels will start teaching from 12:00 pm to 06:00 pm and then again will repeat the tele-cast from 06:00 pm to 12:00 am.

If an average Indian spends ₹ 1,000 monthly and total students are around 40 crores then it will be a saving for citizens of ₹ 5 Lakh crores annually which they can invest anywhere. A separate TV channel will be opened for teaching different sports. Also, a separate TV channel will be opened for moral science where experiential learning and ethics will be taught.

In families where there are more than one child, the elder child can learn on Youtube. If more than one child is younger than 10 years then a monitor will be given to them where 75 per cent cost will be paid by the government as subsidy and 25 per cent will have to be paid by the citizen who will have to pay only ₹ 2,000 for purchase of a monitor. In that monitor, there will either be an inbuilt internet enabled sim or it can be connected with mobile phones and videos can be displayed.

The Data will be collected from telecom operators of how many families have internet data connection and it will be matched with the Aadhar number of families. The Families which do not have any internet data enabled mobile connection. An android mobile phone with 2 GB per day data of one year will be provided to all housewives of those families. Now, the question arises as to how exams will be conducted?

Exams can be conducted in two ways, one is the traditional way in which children will go to their institutions and the second way is online examination. A software will be installed on laptops and this software will record the voice of the student and will take its sample voice and it will be done in the presence of a government teacher. Then once the exam starts, if the student moves his or her eyes from the desktop or keyboard, then his/her exam will be cancelled.

If there is a voice of any family member or anyone except the student during the exam, then also the exam will be cancelled.

Online education will be adopted first either by well educated parents or by very poor families. Then it will be accepted by parents in urban areas and then rural India will adopt it. It will take 5 to 10 years.

After some years, all teachers will be deputed to other departments.

❏

9 Re-engineering Media Processes

*M*edia or press is such an institution that is more powerful than a government. When the government becomes unpopular or more powerful, then it may abdicate its power for some contracts or money.

There are around 10 lakh people employed in journalism in the country. Ninety per cent of them earn only enough that if they will not take part in corruption then they cannot feed their family. Many courts have directed to print media houses to give a good salary package to their employees but media houses do not comply with that order. So in Ramrajya, the government will ensure to provide a good salary to all such media persons and it may cost around ₹ 20,000 crores to the government every year. The guidelines and rules regarding it will be made so that corruption in media can be eliminated.

A Press Trust of India will be made by a constitutional quasi-judicial body by passing a law. The Press Trust of India will submit its report to the central government and demand the amount required to pay the salaries of media persons.

The Media in the hands of businessmen and leaders is detrimental for the nation and its people. But it cannot be undone.

Corporates will be allowed to have major shareholding in the media companies but they will be able to only intervene in revenue matters of media companies. In the matters related to journalism, the owner of the media house will not be able to intervene.

The Press Trust of India will appoint the chief editor of the media house and corporate owner will appoint the CEO of the media house.

Any media house of the country will not be able to accept any advertisement from any government. Instead the general public will have to pay more money to see that media channel.

The owners of the media houses and their family members will not be allowed to take any contract from the government, or any monetary, or any kind of favour from any government.

If it is proved that the corporate has intervened in the journalistic matters of the media channel or newspaper then the whole shareholding of that corporate will be transferred to the Press Trust of India.

The chairman of the Press Trust of India and its members will be elected through online voting. All journalists will be given a license by the central government and journalists who have this license will only be able to vote in the election of the chairman of the Press Trust of India.

❑

10 Re-engineering Administration Process

*I*n India, we are rewarding pliability in a civil servant and honesty is being punished. If an officer is pliable towards political leaders then he would not be accountable towards his duties or towards the general public. He would also not care for his career and promotions, or even for his image in the general public.

The honest officers have been discouraged by the system. When they first join civil services, they start doing such things which the country really needs. But by transferring them, mentally torturing them and threatening them to destroy their career, they force themselves to become adaptable to the system.

Firstly we need to allot KRAs to all civil servants and all employees of the central and all state governments. If the state government does not want to implement it, then the central government can implement it over all IAS, IPS and IRS officers, by issuing a notification through the department of personnel and training or can direct every state government to allocate KRAs.

Or it can be done that 25 per cent KRAs will be allocated by the central government and 75 per cent will be allocated by the state governments. There are many benefits of allocating KRAs to civil servants.

1. If key performance indicators of any civil servant are good then it will be hard for the state government to transfer him frequently.

2. Every civil servant will know that adulation cannot give them promotions but their performance will.

3. There will be gigantic speed in the implementation of the government plans and schemes.

4. There will be a learning website for all civil servants. They would need to complete e-learning lessons every year. Its marks will be added in their confidential report.

5. There will be a suggestion site for all civil servants. They can send their suggestions directly to the chief minister or Prime Minister.

6. There should be a whistle blower site for civil servants.

Every IAS, IPS and IRS will be sent for 15 days training to top business schools of India and the world every year.

Technology and Innovation Department will send the proposal of KRA allotment to the department of personnel and training. After getting the approval, this department will allocate KRAs to all DM, SSP or IAS, IPS and IRS officers. Till the data of government's work does not go online then the score of KRA will be decided on the basis of manual feeding of data results. ❑

11 Re-engineering Banking Process

There are two parts in banking: General Banking and Loan Management. But the most important part is customer service.

How to Improve Customer Service

All public sector banks have now started giving performance linked incentives to their employees. The Finance Ministry can issue these guidelines for public sector banks to improve their customer service:

1. Banks must issue a circular that if there are several misbehaviour complaints in a year against any staff, then that staff will not be eligible for the performance-linked incentive for that year.

2. All banks need to create a public feedback system. Every month banks will analyse the transaction done by every staff where the direct interaction happened with the customer. It will create a list of 25 customers randomly who had transaction with an employee. And this list will be high for Branch Managers. Then the bank will call these customers and take their feedback about the service

and behaviour of the employee. If the bank gets negative feedback about an employee regularly for many months then the bank will call the staff member to the training centre of the bank. There, the senior management officials with a psychotherapist will try to understand the psychological history of that employee by having many hours of discussions with the employee and will try to change that wrong thought process for many days. But even if after such programmes, an employee does not improve his or her behavior then the bank can proceed for punishment. But I believe that they will change.

Do We Need to Privatize Public Sector Banks?

Privatizing public sector banks will not solve any problem but create a much bigger problem for the country. As banking services would be so costly that 85 per cent of the Indian population will not be able to afford the services and financial exclusion will happen. But if we don't privatize then unethical interference may continue by the governments and the NPA problem will keep increasing .

We need to give status like chief of the election commissionner or CAG to chairman of the bank board of India and then transfer all government shareholdings in the public sector banks to the Trust of Bank Board of India.

1. If a customer wants to drop a cheque in drop box then he will scan the cheque from both sides with the scanner available in internet banking app of that bank. Till the image of the cheque is not perfectly captured in the app he will not be able to submit the cheque in the internet banking app. Once filling details of cheque number amount in words and numbers, the beneficiary account number and IFSC code, he will submit the cheque and then drop the cheque in the dropbox of the bank branch. The branch just has to see if it is in order and then approve the queue in CBS and the cheque will reach the paying branch for approval in CTS.

46

2. If a customer of any bank wants to issue a cheque to anybody, he will go to his internet banking app and fill the beneficiary name account number, IFSC code, amount and cheque date and will submit, then a QR code will be generated. This QR code will reflect in the internet banking notifications of the beneficiary. He may scan it and can see all its details, he will not be able to credit the amount before the cheque date. After the cheque due date, he will click on the notification and allow credit then the drawer's account will be debited immediately and the drawee account will be credited. The QR code will only be credited into the same account number and IFSC code which the drawer enters in his internet banking.

3. If anybody needs to withdraw a large amount in cash, and he does not want to wait in the bank line then he will need to login in his internet banking app then he will click on cash payment request. After this, he will fill the amount and name of person who will collect the cash and his Aadhar number. He will select the account to be debited and submit and then enter the OTP number and then submit again. A queue will reach the cashier of that bank branch from where he needs to withdraw money. The cashier will view the transaction details and take a printout of the authority letter automatically sent by the internet banking app and then submit the queue to the accountant or manager of the bank branch. The Manager will authorize the transaction and the queue will reach the cashier. The cashier will wait for the person who will collect cash. When he comes then he will check his Aadhar Number and get his signature on the authority letter and will enter the denomination, submit the document and pay the cash. The authority letter will be treated as a voucher. If anybody has any doubt regarding forgery then the thumb impression verification can be done on the Aadhar site at the time of payment by an officer. The amount will only be debited

after cash is disbursed by the cashier. It will work on the methodology of the green channel counter. Time limits can be set for these transactions.

4. If The general public wants to know how much it has transferred into a specific account in the last year or in the past or how much has come into their account from a specific account in the past, then the bank can give them an option in CBS and internet banking that they can feed from the account number. From the account number they will be able to see the transaction to the specific account or from the specific account in a given period of time.

5. The Bank should give an option to the general population to create 10, 15, 20, 25 and 30 years of fixed deposit. Customers who opt for a 20-year FD should get 0.1 per cent higher rate of interest for every year over the 5 year fixed deposit. If a customer has created a fixed deposit of more than 5-years and if he does premature withdrawal then he will be paid interest at the rate applicable on the length of the term of fixed deposit he has remained with the bank. Or he will be paid interest rate of 5-years FD even if he prematurely withdraws it. After five years or before 10 years he will get an interest rate of 5 years if he prematurely withdraws it after 10 years and before 15 years, he will get interest at the rate of 10-years FD and so on. It will solve the asset and liability mismatch problem of banks and then the bank will have free money for long-term loans.

6. The Chief technology and innovation department will find the PAN No. of all Aadhar holders through facial, address and mobile no. scan. Once they get this data then it will direct the banks to convert all those jandhan accounts into regular SB accounts and feed PAN no. from the backend. People who are found without a PAN no., they will be issued a PAN card on the basis of this Aadhar card and the PAN card will be sent to the address given in the Aadhar card.

Loan Management Solutions

Automation of Loan Processing and Sanctioning Process

1. **Agriculture Loans :** There are around 14 crore hectares of agriculture land out of which in my view only three crore or four crore hectares land have bank KCC. Now, the government will ask the Bank Board to sanction loans as per the agri-land records link with one Aadhar which does not already have KCC. Thus, KCC will be sanctioned on twelve crore hectares of land to around ten crore farmers. In this way, thirty lakh crores of advances will be sanctioned within one month and get disbursed within six months.

First, in the loans will be sanctioned automatically either by the corporate centres of the banks or Bank Board of India. The branch manager or field officers just have to open the website, download the documents, get them signed by the farmer and select the disbursed option and submit them automatically. The loan will get disbursed and charge on the land will automatically be noted. Second question, if the farmer had already availed the KCC? To know this a software will be run where the farmer's cibil will be scanned and it can be seen or determined that he has KCC already or not. The Stamp duty will be waived by all governments on these loans. Now the question arises that without application from a farmer, how can the loan be sanctioned? Yes, the loan can be sanctioned but if a farmer fails to complete documentation within six months then the loan will be cancelled by the bank automatically. If a farmer wants to refuse the loan, then he can visit any branch and give his Aadhar number and thumb impression and the loan will be cancelled.

Now, the question arises that every rural branch of the country will have an average around 2000 extra KCC accounts and banks don't have sufficient staff to follow up. Then what we will do is we will give only 90 per cent amount in KCC and the remaining 10 per cent in interest repayment account.

An interest repayment account will be automatically opened with KCC. Before one year of disbursement, interest will be automatically credited into the KCC account from this interest repayment account. Renewal will not be necessary by changing the laws. After the government announces the MSP, all limits will be automatically increased as per the MSP and provision for this will be made in documentation. It will be a lifelong KCC account. Every year limit will increase by 10%.

2. **SME Loans:** The Bank Board of India will create a list of all the current accounts which have more than 5 crores of average credit summations in the last 5 years and will run the Cibil of their proprietors, partners and directors and then ask the bank board to offer them loans. A website will be made especially for this purpose. An email with a link will be sent to all such current account holders. When they open it, then they will be shown the limits to offer. If they click on yes then their properties all over India linked with their Aadhar will be shown to them with the valuation as per the circle rate. Then they have to choose which property to offer and they will be asked if they need a term loan or cash credit. After selecting this option, they will be asked to go through a video confirmation and Aadhar authentication. After doing so, the loan will be sanctioned by the corporate centre or bank board. Then the branch just has to download the documents and get them signed by the customer after disbursal. The Charge will be automatically noted on the properties and CERSAI. In this way, we can easily disburse 50 lakh crores. This will be done when the balance sheet and ITR are linked with each other.

In the SME account, if interest is not paid on time even after good sales the interest and EMI portion will be added into the tax liabilities of the enterprise. The government will be able to forcefully take it from the borrower by attaching his assets and then giving it to the banks.

3. **Retail Loans:** When all government departments have their own HRMS then data will be integrated with banks including

current posting of the employee and his present address and salary.

The employees who have been employed for more than a year, after integration of CIBIL, some notifications in their internet banking informing that they are eligible for this amount of personal loan, car loan or housing loan.

For personal loan, after clicking on the notification and submitting the required amount, a queue will be generated to the corporate centre. The loan will get sanctioned within two hours and then the customer has to go to the branch for documentation.

After the documentation, branch will click on disbursal and submit it, immediately the amount will be disbursed and lien on GPF and other funds will be marked of the customer.

4. **For Car Loans:** The Parivahan Ministry of the central government will allot a unique identification number to all car dealers, auto-dealers, and bike-dealers operating in India. The customer just has to click on the notification to see if he is eligible for car loan.

The government will allot a unique identification number to all car models and all variants of cars, bikes and autos. The Banks will update this data into their software. The customer will have to enter the car model, unique identification number and car dealer's unique identification number and then he has to scan the quotation and upload it. Now he has to fill the amount of loan he requires, the amount he has already paid and the amount he will pay on delivery, and then the customer only submit, papers not required to write.

Then, a queue will reach the concerned dealer. The dealer will inform the bank on which date he can deliver, he has issued this quotation or not and what amount he has got as advance payment, and then he will submit. Then the queue will reach the corporate centre of the bank, and the loan will get sanctioned within two hours. As the loan gets sanctioned, customer will get a message and he will go to the branch for documentation. There, he will complete documentation and then the branch official will click on disbursal and submit the amount from his saving account and loan will be disbursed. An email containing all the required forms which are already signed digitally by the bank official will be sent to the dealer.

5. **For Housing Loans:** TIR will not be needed as all information and history of land will be available online on the bank's intranet. As the agriculture land will be made a part of the SARFAESI Act, valuation will not be needed.

Question: Valuations as per circle rate of land shows only value of land. If there is a construction, how will it be added into the valuation report?

Answer: The bank will stop accepting the valuation report from valuers. As the businessman or retail customer accepts the offer of loan, suddenly an email and WhatsApp message with location of properties on the mobile of field officers will be sent by the bank. The field officer will immediately visit the property and take photos so that in these photos the entire area of the property will be covered and then he will upload it on the bank's PSS software and will also feed the carpet area and vacant area. The bank's corporate centre will mark the construction from level 1 to 10 and then actual valuation of property will be displayed.

Once, TIR and valuation are not needed, then the housing loan sanction process will be expedited.

NPA:

1. Notices to NPA and SMA or irregular account will be sent at the central level. An office in every circle of every bank will be created for sending the notices.

That is why, I want banks to create a software where notices will be made automatically as an account becomes irregular or NPA. Then people in the circle of the central office will print the notices, sign and send them. An email containing the notices, speed post number and receipt by borrower will be mailed to the concerned branch mail and will also be saved in the branch FTP.

2. The government need not recapitalize the public sector banks. Instead government must purchase mortgaged properties of defaulters with this money with two clauses.

   1. The government will not sell these properties before ten years of the purchasing date.

   2. After ten years, these properties will not be sold at less than 150 per cent of the purchasing price. The Government can issue the real estate government bonds and can purchase these properties from banks in large numbers. For banks, it will be a recovery and not write off.

If the government does not want to do so, then it can create a statutory body and banks will provide money which is kept as provision to this company either as loan or investment. Then this company will purchase these properties from banks. The two clauses mentioned above will be a part of it too.

❑

12 Corruption Control Mechanism

There will be a corruption intelligence unit. Initially there will be recruitment of 10,000 officers.

There will be a Revenue Intelligence Unit that will acquire information about tax theft by the individuals and corporates.

Both these intelligence units will submit their reports to a central committee which will consist of 50 per cent of civil society members, Chief Justice of India, Prime Minister and all Chief Ministers.

An Anti Corruption Bureau in all states will keep functioning.

Initially all offices of IAS and IPS will be under survillance for the chief minister's control room. The Chief Minister can monitor the offices any time.

After six months of its implementation, all offices of the state governments will be made online to the office of District Magistrates and SSPS and to the chief minister's office. The audio can also be made live in future.

A central helpline toll-free number will be available for people. People can call on this number and can provide corruption details from anywhere in the country. Names and phone numbers of such citizens will be kept secret and this helpline will provide details of such corruption to an officer. The officer of the corruption intelligence unit will start investigation silently and will arrange proof, and then he will submit the report to the corruption control committee. Then this committee will issue a warrant and that person will be arrested. Once the corrupt officers start getting arrested all over the country then there will be a fear in the minds of the corrupt people. The Cases of such corrupt people will be heard by the judges appointed by the Corruption Control Committee.

For controlling corruption, there should be two things needs to be implemented.

1. Most of the discretion powers held by the officers in the country should be reduced to minimum level. If a citizen is eligible for some service then there should be no discretion power with the officer to deny him the service.

2. All the services provided by the state governments and central governments will be made online and human intervention should be reduced to the minimum level.

There are 11,830 kinds of services that the central and state governments provide. We need to bring all these services on one government portal and for that a system like core banking solution is needed.

All kinds of taxes should be made through an online android application. Nobody should go to the bank for depositing a challan. On this app you can pay advance income tax. You can file your income tax return and you can also select the service of any state government. Then the challan category will be automatically selected. You need to pay the challan from your account through net banking or through debit card or credit card. Then after a successful payment a challan receipt will be generated and you will have to provide that receipt to the government authorities. A system will be added by the banks through which the government authorities will be able to enquire credit or debit transactions by challan number or journal number. An email of receipt will be automatically sent to the concerned officer of the government department as well as to the email ID of the depositor.

The GST collection will be made online if anybody purchases anything. If he pays through debit card, credit card or net banking then the GST amount in the bill will automatically be deducted from the account of seller and will be transferred to the government account. When most of the data of the nation is online, then the government will issue an ATM card to all Aadhar card holders. If they spend more than ₹ 5,000 on anything in cash, then they will have to show this card to the POS machine and Aadhar data with transaction data will be saved on the government website.

If somebody purchases something for more than ₹ 5,000 in cash then the GST amount will be automatically deducted from the current account with OD facility of seller and will get transferred to the state government and central government account. So, there will not be any need for the seller to file GST return. The GST return will be automatically sent to the email ID of the seller at midnight of the last day of the month. The central government will not need to give the states governments their share. The seller will deposit the entire cash into his current account.

There will not be any need for processing the GST refund. It will also be automatic, as sale of the product occurred at the retail counter.

There are so many kinds of corruption in the country. Some major corruption areas that I need to mention are:

1. Roads, highways and other such infrastructure project's expenditure throughout the country was around 20 lakh crores every year before corona happened, In these projects a significant number of corruption may be involved. The project's cost is increased so that the commission can be paid to bureaucrats and politicians. As per my estimate there

may be corruption of around 5-6 lakh crores every year and it can be ended by declaring a maximum project's cost per kilometre as per the length and width of roads and highways.

There are around 30 lakh crores of registry done in the whole country before the corona period. Citizens are asked for 2 per cent which means around 60,000 crores of corruption may exist per year in all registrar offices in the country.

There are thousands of crores of corruption every year in police departments in India.

There are thousands of crores of corruption in transfer of civil servants all over the country and there is an immense possibility that this money reaches from down to top.

All this corruption can be ended by innovation and technology.

When land records are updated with Aadhaar number, a letter by tax authorities will be sent to every purchaser of land asking from where they had arranged the money for purchasing the land for more than a certain amount in the last 20 years. They will have to reply within 3 months otherwise they will be charged 5 per cent for delay of every three months of the value as per the circle rate of the land. If they fail to pay the amount, then it will be deducted by the sub-registrar from the sale value of the land whenever in future they sell the land. When the citizens' information profile is created then professional details and history of every individual will also be updated and all designations like politicians, contractors businessmen, and chartered accountants. Everybody who is having high probability to have more black money will receive the notice first asking them from where the money came for purchasing the land.

The government may get 50 lakhs crores of tax collection by doing so and making these land records digitilize will have an expenditure of ₹ 2,500 crores.

How to Counter Black Money within the Country?

Answer: Many ways have been mentioned above but one last and very effective way is here:

The RBI provides cash to currency chest branches of all banks. When RBI sends currency then the number of notes are mentioned in the letter with denomination of notes. The serial number of the note's series will be mentioned there. The banks need to make provision in their CBS that they enter the denomination in their vault in CBS, they will need to enter from this note number to this note number. Then when they give the cash to cash officer or cash officers give it to branches or cashiers, then they will need to enter the serial no. of the note's that are given to the cashier or branch.

Then the banks will ask manufacturers of note counting machines to attach a scanner with the note counting machine. When the cashier counts the notes before withdrawal or deposit the note number will be captured and while doing withdrawal or deposit those number of notes will be allocated into the PAN of the customer or Adhaar number of the customer. Initially this provision can be made for notes of denomination of ₹ 50 and above.

When a citizen purchases anything costing more than ₹ 5000 in cash then the shopkeeper will count these notes on the same note counting machines and add the Adhaar or PAN of the customer. Currency tracking will happen and most of the genuine population will do online transactions or payment. And corruption will decrease.

❏

13 Re-engineering Employment Process

The government will ask for business ideas from the citizens of the country and then will analyse all these ideas and their scope in the domestic and international market.

The government with the help of IIMs and all big businesses will conduct a survey. This survey will classify citizens as per their present purchasing power capacity and the government will ask Google to provide data of interests of Indians for different products.

A survey will be conducted to know about such domestic products where by increasing the quality or by lowering the price, citizens would like to purchase the product. Then after finding it, the government will ask interested corporates and citizens to produce such products at a lower price and with high-quality.

For start-ups, the government will create a national portal where every individual can send his idea of business and it will be shown to all venture capitalists' companies and top 1,000 companies of India and the world. If any company likes the idea and wants to invest money in the project then it can directly talk to the entrepreneur.

The country has 150 crores of population it means 30 crore families and the government's target would be to provide 30 crores employment at the first stage of development six crores are employed in the private sector and public sector. Twenty-four crores should be employed in Agriculture, MSME and other sectors as labours.

We need to support 5 lakh ideas every year with support of ₹ 100,000 to 1 crore and regular mentoring of entrepreneur till 3 years will be done. The target should be that every entrepreneur will employ a minimum of 100 people within five years. Advertisement expenditure of all such entrepreneurs will be spent by government from government funds whether it is domestic or international. Technical, psychological and emotional support will be provided by the government till they become profitable and self capable.

By ensuring a certain MSP on every agriculture product youngster will move towards agriculture and they will be encouraged to shift their crops which are more profitable and demand more labour and technical support. Crops which get destroyed by the natural calamities, farmers will get compensation by increasing 2 per cent selling price which means 12 per cent above MSP. For 60,000 crores every year, farmers will get compensation for crop destruction without paying a single rupee for crop insurance.

Government must talk to the USA and European countries for work visas for around 5 crore Indians. India can easily employ 5 crore Indians as carpenters and plumbers. Housekeepers and can easily earn 1,500 dollars per month there. If they are able to send 200 dollars per month to their family or parents then their family can survive easily and their security and other factors will be the responsibility of the Indian embassy and Indian government. Indian foreign reserves will get an addition of 120 billion dollars. After serving for some years they can return and start a business with the money they save there.

The unemployed citizens who can't get employed abroad or don't have agriculture land to grow crops will be eligible to get employed in MNREGA. If they work for 180 days then it will be deemed that they have worked for 240 days and sixty days wages will be deposited in their PF accounts own which they can withdraw after 5 years. With that money they can start their business or repay any loan .

Initially only 5 crore citizens will get employment in MNREGA. It will cost around ₹ 24,000 crores. After completion of the economic census, MNREGA work will be allocated to one person in a family of lowest economic category E.

One way to increase jobs is job credits to corporates. It will be like job credits. If a corporate provides 1000 jobs in his company then as per salary and designation of employee 25 per cent salary will be given to him as job credit. The government can take responsibility of the whole PF continuation of employee and employer.

One more way to upskill working or general class of population is that the skill development ministry will create a website and an app, wherein youngsters will login and will give an aptitude and language test and then select a particular position in a specific sector or company. Then this app will provide the user all written and verbal video material online and will keep taking his tests and finally when the user is ready, the government will arrange for interviews or internships.

❑

14 Re-engineering Social Processes

There are many evils in the society of the world and no politician or political ideology is able to correct or eliminate these evils. They work on deep emotional levels and are inherited by human beings since their birth. Some examples of society's evil are races and castes system, non-vegetarianism, careless attitude towards mother earth and towards its weak inhabitants and resources.

The solution for all these evils is only a sub-religion like religion of humanity. The question is how will it eliminate all these evils?

Answer is:- There are several crores of people out of 700 crores of population who are very progressive and thinks that all these evils must be eliminated.

All religions have a deity God or a son of God, but this religion does not have any deity, God or a son of God then how will it succeed?

Answer is:- That whoever accepts religion of humanity will remove his surname or will add human at the place of surname or after his surname.

In this way the caste system will end within fifty years as nobody will be able to know who belongs to which caste.

Anybody who accepts religion of humanity will not need to change his religion, and can continue with his religion. He or she will only have to follow some principles of human religion of humanity. Such are:

1. He or she will have to be a complete vegetarian. He can only have eggs.

2. He will be allowed to have a maximum of two children and if he wishes to contribute to the world then he can have one child of his own and adopt one child.

3. Whatever he earns and accumulates in his life, if it is more than a certain limit then he will have to donate 50 per cent of his wealth before transferring it to his children.

4. He will have a duty to plant one thousand trees for every family member of his family.

5. He will never believe that anybody is a degraded human being on the basis of religion, race, caste, money, power, position or authority.

6. He will try hard to forego any ego in his heart raised due to wealth, power, position, authority, or intelligence.

7. He will always stand with truth. If he has to lose something due to that, he will happily lose.

8. He will keep himself away from illegal and immoral money throughout his life and will teach the same to his children.

9. He will address the population of the world as mother, father, brother, sister and lover in his personal life and it will make the whole world one family and a beautiful place to live in.

Women's Reservation Bill

If you want to reform a society then give equal rights, opportunity, representation and power to women as it is given to men. The government will bring 50 per cent Women Reservation Bill to legislative assembly, Lok Sabha, Rajya Sabha and public services in parliament and will get it passed. The nation will change positively within 15 years.

Reservation Bill as Per Population Ratio and Economic Status

Reservation is not a poverty alleviation programme. It is a way to give representation to weak castes in society so that they can live with dignity and without fear and humiliation. If reservation system wasn't there then would social status and dignified life for people of lower castes have been possible and would have we expected the parliament to make such strong laws in favour of SC and ST?

So, the government should get this bill passed in parliament. And caste and religions will get their share of reservation that they have in population in the central government and state government jobs.

Population Control Bill

The government will get this law passed. As per this law, no individual will be allowed to have more than two children after exactly one year of the enactment of this law. People who will not follow this law, may face imprisonment of three months with 5 per cent more tax rate for their whole life and will not be eligible for any benefits by the government.

Uniform Civil Code

The government will get this law passed.

Establishment of Anti-Human Trafficking Agency and Anti-Forced Prostitution Agency.

These agencies will eliminate social disasters and the government will free all girls and women working as bonded sex workers by the use of CRPF and then will provide ₹ 20000 to them per month for their whole life as compensatory pension due to the failure of government. A whole city will be constructed for all girls and women whom government will free from bonded sex work.

A city will be constructed for childrens who are begging on streets and here they will be educated and sheltered.

A city will be constructed for senior citizens whose childrens have abandoned them who don't have food and shelter with them?

There are 80 lakh blind people in the country. To give them vision, the country will need to spend 2 lakh crores. The government will spend this amount in five years which means 40,000 crores every year.

Everyone who is handicapped will be provided with artificial organs at the expense of the government. The government will spend 10,000 crores every year for it.

The government will allocate ₹ 13,000 crores every year for food for stray animals and will ensure a corruption free system to make it reach beneficiaries.

If a child who has any major ailment since birth, then the government will fully sponsor his treatment and for that 20,000 crores every year will be spent.

And for all such things, expenditure of around 1 lakh crore will be arranged by increasing the value and profit of all public sector undertakings.

❑

15 How to Finance All Suggestions

The total tax collection of all states, union territories and central government was around 56 lakh crores before the corona period. If we consider 4 per cent fiscal deficit for the central government and average the same for the state government then the total budget expenditure would be around 70 lakh crores. Around 40 per cent meaning 28-30 lakh crores are spent on salaries, perks, pensions, maintenance and administrative expenses. Around 9 lakhs crores are spent on interest payments. Out of the remaining 31 lakh crores, 20 lakh crores spent on roads, highways, bridges and infrastructure projects. As for the remaining 11 lakh crores, there are many social sector schemes like public distribution system, direct benefit transfer to widows, old aged, disabled and farmers, MNAREGA, etc. So, very little money is left to be spent on health and justice infrastructure.

For solutions of agri distress government would no need to spent a rupee from its budget.

For the public funding of elections, the government would need 65000 crores for five years which means 13,000 crores every year for all state and central elections and it can be done either by imposing election cess with income tax and corporate income tax or by imposing ₹ 2 as tax on petrol and diesel.

For implementation of suggestions on judiciary, government would need to invest 100,000 crores for infrastructure and 25,000 crores and 20,000 crores every year on salaries of added judges and supporting staff for Infrastructure, government can impose 50-50 ratio for central government and states. If the state governments do not agree to give their share then it must be considered which government wants more to see positive changes happen.

If central government wants to see more positive change happen and thinks that responsibility for the nation is first then they must allocate funds for this infrastructure and should bear the burden of salaries.

For implementation of suggestions on education, central government needs only 5,000 crores from central funds and it can be easily done.

We need one pistol for every police constable and funds of 20,000 crores can be arranged in 50:50 share of central and state governments. ₹ 5 lakhs for every thana and police chowkies within the area of that thana it will cost around 9,000 crores every year. It should also be done by central government funds for all other technological changes government needs to invest only few thousands crores. It can either be done by state governments or the central governments.

For technological changes in administration only 2,000 to 3,000 crores will be required.

For controlling corruption, government will need to invest only 5,000 crores annually.

For banking reforms government can issue real estate bonds and can purchase assets of borrowers sold by banks with this money.

For implementation of solutions in health care of the country. government would need to invest 3 lakh crores one time and 30,000 crores annually on salaries and 5,000 crores annually on maintenance so government can ask the state governments on how much they wish to share. I think planned expenditure of 12 lakh crores of central government can be used as six lakh crores for judiciary, healthcare and employment for only one year and the remaining six lakh crores for all other ministries and schemes.

For implementation of suggestions on employment.

MNREGA expenditure will be 240,000 crores. It must be shared with states on 50:50 bases which means 120,000 crores for central government.

If there are 20 lakh jobs added every year by the private sector then if they pay one lakh rupees per month average to an employee then 50,000 crores of provision should be made for job credits.

For six lakh crores 120,000+50,000+145,000+330,000+ 29,000+5,000= 679,000 crores.

All these suggestions will get implemented by providing 679,000 crores for only one year or the first year.

❏

16 Re-engineering Thought Process

Human Life

Part 1

Human psychology is made up of belief systems and belief systems are made up of experiences. If someone remains with a belief system for a longer time, then he gets attached to it deeply. How often someone recall the belief system determines the level of attachment to it.

For example:-

When a child is born, he does not know that this is his mother or this is his father. He even does not know the meaning of mother and father. He sees his mother with wonder thinking "who is this person". Mother smiles at him, mother hugs him and breastfeeds him. Then the child realises that this person feeds me when I am hungry, and after several such acts the child get attached to his mother. He feels love for his mother, as his mother feels for him. The child also does not know that this is his father. When his father plays with him with toys, the child smiles and feels that this person entertains me often. When it occurs regularly then the child gets attached to his father. When the child grows up, his mother tells him that "this is your grandmother, this is your grandfather, this is your uncle, this is your aunt, this is your brother, this is your sister," etc. The child creates a belief system of it as it has been created for his parents.

Everybody keeps calling him with a name, he develops a belief system that this is me or this is my name. Soon as he grows parents take him to their place of worship and tell him that he is God and you have to worship him. He asks, "what does God do" and he is being told that god is the creator of the universe. This sky, this land, and everyone worships him; your parents worship him. The story is regarding the religion and religious books are told to him. A belief system develops in his mind that this is God. He was not told that there are so many religions and Ram, Allah, WaheGuru, Jesus,Mahatma Buddh, Mahavir are all God or sons of God and they are worshipped by other religions even when he grows up. Since birth he had a belief that only his god is God and no one else.

Soon he is told about their caste, race, etc. and he creates a belief system about his caste and race.

Age from 5 to 15 Years-

At this age whatever they see, hear or experience in their family, they paint their whole inner world with these colours of sanskars and see the world with these perspectives.

If there are clashes in the family due to father, mother, grandparents or anyone, and whatever is told to them by the person whom they love most, creates a belief system in them that this person is not good, and they start hating him, because at this age they operate through their heart and not through their mind as they are too sensitive.

Whatever is told to a child at this age stays with him throughout his life. As an example, if you tell them that eating non-veg is good, everybody eats in the family and if you feed them then they will turn to be a non-vegetarian throughout their life. If there are clashes due to lack of money between parents or family members then the thought process of a child will be more towards survival or to support his family monetarily. But if there is abundance of money then the thought process of a child will be more towards dreams. He will see short-term dreams. It is the responsibility of parents to know the strength and interests of their child and persuade them to have a long-term dream of their interest. At this age, the dream of child won't have content of youth aspiration. And youth has the capability to distract the child.

Fulfilling every wish of your child makes him more dependent on you psychologically and it deprives him of opportunities where he need to be on his own.

The child does what he sees his parents doing when it comes to ethics. What you teach your child and what you do in your daily life are two different things. At this age the child become familiar with most important words in a person's life like career, struggle, corruption, ethics, respect, peace and love. The depth of commitment in the mind of a child to this word 'career' is determined by the behaviour of his parents.

Whether a child is ready to face struggles or not to fulfil his dreams or requirement is also determined by the daily behaviour of his parents. Either they make the child strong or weak.

Their attitude towards Corruption, peace and love is also been learnt through the parents' behaviour.

Age from 16 to 23

At 16, children experience adolescence in their body and mind. Adolescence brings too much enthusiasm in children's life. Adolescence adds a flavour of youthful aspirations into children's dream. Sometimes their dreams change due to these youthful aspirations. In most of the cases adolescence brings negative changes into one's personality, specially for boys.

The friends circle becomes very important at this age. Thoughts of friends impact a child in such a way that he sometimes unlearns the teachings of his parents and teachers. Adolescence brings a kind of artificiality in a child's personality. He behaves in a different way and walks in a different way in front of the opposite sex. He sometimes uses the wealth or power of his parents to attract the opposite sex.

Children at this age want respect and appreciation from everybody due to their adolescence. Ego first comes in adolescence. At this age boys become aggressive and girls become shy due to adolescence.

Children at this age have misconceptions about love. They are not able to differentiate between love and attraction. They get attracted to someone and they start believing that they love them.

At this age, so many desires take birth in a child's mind inspired by his classmates, relatives or environment.

He becomes selfish at this age and his focus is on fulfilling these desires. These desires are distracting.

And children who are unable to continue their studies due to these desires harm their future in the long run.

This is the age when the real development of the mind happens, foundation of career is made, and foundation of principles is laid. This is the most important time in someone's life as at this age the future and thoughts gets shape.

There is a common pattern of thoughts in youths at this age and they all believe that they have a lot of time to study or to build a career.

Most of the time decisions about a career are taken very late which harms the future of a child. And sometimes decisions about a career are taken very early without considering that the interests of the child could change in future. Thus, money and energy of the child and family gets wasted.

One of the most important reasons of failure of a child in future is addiction at this age. If a child gets addicted to alcohol, smoking, tobacco, etc. then there remains only 50 per cent chances of success for such a child.

In a country's working class there are three kinds of workers.

First—Upper-class children who after completing their studies manage the business of their parents.

Second—Lower and middle-class children who complete their studies and find a job in public or private enterprise.

Third—Lower-class children who cannot complete their studies due to poverty or distractions. They are unable to build a career, and in the long run mafias and criminals are born out of these children and they harms the society.

Unemployment of youths is very dangerous for a country's future as unemployed youth can easily be diverted to illegal and harmful activities to fulfil their requirements and ambitions. If they are in large number then the gravity of the problem will be severe.

Age from 23 to 30

At this age the youngsters become too worried about their future. Some complete their masters in different streams and try to get a good job in the private sector; some aspire for the government jobs and start having coaching classes. Though some don't have resources but they still believe that they can manage and they do self–study.

These individuals continue their struggle for their career and a select few get success while others few get failure. Most of those who fail opt for self-employment, and once settled most of them get married.

Even the individuals who have been employed get married by the age of 30.

At the age of 30, the individuals have some common regrets like my friend, batchmate or classmate has reached that level and I am still here; or his wife or her husband is too smart but mine is not. Till this age individuals become independent or settled.

Age from 30 to 45

At this age, the individuals work hard to reach a higher level in career and get busy in their married life. This is the period when individuals try hard to build their own house and purchase their own car, not everybody but many of them succeed in achieving these dreams. They spend money on their children's primary and secondary education. At this age, the individuals allow themselves to enjoy their life. Individuals who never had any addiction get addicted in this period.

If hard work on education is not done between the age of 16 to 23, then it would seriously affect your life later between the age of 30 to 45. It create happiness when they achieve their dreams and then they raise the level of their dreams. But individuals of labour class get very depressed at this age because after labour of the whole day, they don't get enough money to can educate their children or take care of their family. They get depressed and this negativity can be seen in their attitude.

Age from 45 to 60

For some individuals this time is the peak of their career and for some this time is the toughest time of their lives. The fortunate ones spend their money on higher studies of their children. They save money for the marriage of their daughters. They get their children highly educated, employed and then married. Thus, gets relieved from their responsibilities.

On the other hand, the unfortunate ones are not able to educate their children well fulfil rightful demands of their children. Their body does not support their work pressure but they somehow manage. About the age of 45, youth of a person starts withering away and he has a sense of altruism in his personal life. At this time, ego and ambition are the only factors which control altruism.

People who struggle financially, learn the path of dishonesty between the age of 30 to 45 and 45 to 60 in many cases.

Age from 60 to 75

People in services retire at the age of 60. For a few days after retirement they feel good at home but soon they realize that they need to be employed. Many of them try to get employed in some job or opt self-employment but most of them don't find any job or time at home, as due to health issues most of them feel incapable. At this age, people get busy with social media and hobbies but the level of their happiness depends on the support of their children.

But some unfortunate ones can't retire. They keep labouring and support their needs. One day comes when they fall ill and die due to lack of money to spend on the treatment of illness.

Part 2

Present six examples, please read and understand.

Example No. 1— When the upbringing of a child happens in financial distress and he does not get better educational facilities. Then by the age of 20, his aim is to get a good job whether in the public sector or private sector to fulfil the basic requirements of his family. After many years of struggle, he is selected in a company where he works hard and gets respect from his seniors. He is good with customers and good with his seniors. He never thought of leaving the job to start his own business as he had seen so much financial distress in his family and he does not want to take a risk, he remains satisfied with his job.

Example No. 2— The second case is of an individual whose upbringing was not in financial distress but when he completes his education his father tells him to find a job for livelihood. He make efforts and get selected in a company. This is a government job. Here he realised that if you don't work properly, you will still get your salary.

He does only what is necessary. He does not like to learn a new skill. He does not let any chance pass where he can accept money from the company. He is not a good worker. He feels that earning money outside is too difficult so his aim is to gain money from everything so that he would get a good corpus at the time of retirement. These kinds of people are very miserly in their personal and professional life.

Example No. 3— The third kind of people are those whose education could not be completed due to financial distress or ignorance of their parents. They themselves did not focus on education and when they feel that they can't survive they turned to labour. These people are from the labour class and many of them are painters, carpenters, daily wagers, etc.

Example No. 4— Fourth kinds of people are those whose upbringing was done in abundance. They did not focus on study after wasting so many years in enjoying their youth. They participated in their family business but they failed.

Example No. 5— The fifth case is of individual whose upbringing was done in abundance but the discipline was maintained. The parents imparted good teaching to these children and as they grow up they own their family business and thrive on it.

Example No. 6— The sixth case is of a child whose childhood passed without education and he had to earn his living since childhood. He sold tea, snacks, etc. Later, he started some other business and became a rich man. But for him honesty is not important only survival and progress is important. All mafias or people who are involved in illegal trade activities come from such a background. Later most of these people become politicians, and lives in societies where poverty prevails but morals and integrity can't.

Part 3

Human being can be categorized in the following 3 categories:

1. **Self-loving** – These kind of people are selfish people. They do not care for the society and they don't even care for their family. They are always obsessed with their needs and aspirations. They have less integrity.

2. **Family-loving** – These kind of people only care for themselves and their family. They want to give the best possible comfort to their family. These people don't care for the society and have lesser chance to be corrupt than the self-loving persons.

3. **Society-loving** – These kind of people care for the whole society as well as their family. There are no chances of corruption done by these people. They are full of compassion. These kinds of people are very few in the society. They become more successful as they feel the need of society as the need of theirselves. They dream big and they achieve big, whereas self-loving person spends his money on luxuries or self needs.

Human Mind

Part 1- Open mind and Closed mind

Open minded people have higher ambitions, and it makes them unrealistic. They live their lives to impress others to get praise or recognition. Their lives soon becomes artificial as their lives to become idealistic. Open mind is open to dreams, wishes and fears. Open minded people feel less determination in facing challenges. Open mind wait for the perfect environment or circumstances.

Open minded people focus on idealism. Such people do not speak rudely to anybody when it is necessary. Person with open mind feel a great pain within themselves. Soon, this pain makes them depressed and inactive in their personal life. But such persons keep showing that they are well. Open minded people are more creative than closed minded people. Open minded people with favourable circumstances can create inventions.

A closed minded person does not see big dreams. He remains satisfied with his working life and tries to make small efforts so that his salary can be increased. He behaves in a natural way, he does not let any fear of the outside world enter into his mind. Closed minded people remains silent and restricts themselves to voice their opinion. Open minded person has a vision for his life and he thinks that his mental capabilities are extraordinary and he remains in this ego. Open minded people are very emotional and they hardly forget any bad experience.

In my point of view open-minded people can survive only in education and creative field but in the real world only closed minded people can survive. If an open-minded person has to survive then he will survive with a lot of pain. May be there are chances of suicide attempts by such a person.

Part 2

Dreams, Innovation and Intentions

It is said several times that we must have big dreams but big dreams can only be seen with an open mind. Big dreams and big expectations forces the mind to wander into the unknown and while roaming into the unknown you find the solution of the problem or innovation. But for innovation and accuracy you must have basic knowledge and experience in the area of the problem. If you don't have knowledge and experience then you may not find the right innovation. Innovations can only happen when you are at peace there is no worry in your mind and you have a deep desire to solve the problem. Sometimes, praise works as motivation for innovation. I want every student to take a problem, collect the whole information and experiences related with the problem and start doing what you like most. Go deep into this bliss, imagine the dream that it will be fulfilled after the problem is solved. Imagine all the praise, fame, money and public appreciation after the problem is solved and soon you will get the innovation.

Negativity

Negativity is an emotion which is responsible for pessimism in a person regarding a situation, a task, an organization, life, etc. A negative person believes that he can't do this, no one can do this, and everything is bad in an organization, family, country or the whole world.

Negativity is the outcome of failure, disappointments, betrayal, etc. Negativity works in life since birth. Owing to the problem of family, society or country one can be so negative that his perspective and his negativity creates conflict in his personal and professional life and growth.

Whenever we start a task or work and fail, then negativity comes in. When each time we fail in that task or in several works, then we turn so negative. We feel that we are unworthy and we can't do anything and then our targets are always smaller than our abilities and we don't participate in most of the work thinking that we will not succeed and that failure is certain. When a person turns so negative then he become inactive. Due to his attitude and activities, he becomes disreputable in his organization and society. It makes him ultra negative. Negativity in such measure is harmful for mental health and it creates so many disorders in his mind. Soon, if not taken seriously it destroys that person.

Every kind of negativity has its history. If someone is negative about marriage then there must be some history of marital conflicts in his family close relations, friends circle, etc.

In developing countries people are very negative about some public sector organizations because there is a history of corruption, and disrespect to the common citizens.

Failure can happen in any area of one's life and one can turn negative about any sphere of one's life.

Part 1

Negative Perception and Negative Reality

Negativity can be categorized in two ways. First is negative reality and second is negative perception. Negative reality means a situation or person is actually negative and we are negative about them. Negative perception means that the situation or person is negative so we are negative about them and the situation or person is not so negative but we are extremely negative about them. Negative perception can also be caused when the reality is positive but perception is negative. Negative reality is good and it is possible to change. But negative perception is easy to change as it has to be changed in one's mind. Positive perception can turn into negative perception with over thinking. Sometimes negative perception which is not based on truth, creates due to politics of leaders of a country, media or employees of an organization.

Sometimes politics create the reality to change the perception but once perception starts giving benefit to politics then politics does not let it change the perception even though there are many positive changes in the reality. It is evident in many nations and companies.

Part 2

Ego and extremism are the extended hand of negativity.

Someone said anything in excess is poison but I say anything in excess if not controlled is negative and dangerous to the person who holds it. See if you have lot of money then you would surely feel ego but if you don't control and reject it, it will be harmful for not only for your growth but it will be dangerous for the society.

Similarly if you have power, you would surely feel ego over it. But if you don't control or reject that ego, it will change your behaviour in a negative way and will destroy you in the long run. There are many examples of politicians, bureaucrats, businessmen, kings and emperors before us.

If you are beautiful, you would surely feel proud of it but if you don't control or reject it, it will change your personality and affect your future negatively.

If you have authority then you would surely be boastful about it, but if you don't control or reject it, it will surely destroy your growth and everybody will reject you.

Why does ego kill growth?

Because ego does not let you see the real picture and you suddenly start acting on a whim which is why egoistic people are less capable to take the right decision in their personal or professional life. When they take a wrong decision then it kills their growth. Ego is the extended hand of negativity.

What is extremism??

Extremism is an ultra ego of power or money. It normally takes birth from the world 'revenge' but sometimes it becomes more than that. Extremism says if you hurt me than I will hurt you or if you hurt my ego with even your dissent than I will also hurt you.

Extremism is of two kinds—

One that you have makes me a loss of such thing that I lost the ability to forgive you.

Second if you try to insult me, try to fight against my power or even express your dissent to my decisions than you will not be forgiven.

The First kind of extremism, we find in riots. People of a particular community have killed the people of the other community due to extremism or unsocial elements organized to start the riot. Family members of the killed person lose the ability to forgive, they gather and go to the area of the other community and kill anybody whom they see and then they feel satisfied. They do not think, if we are killing the same person who killed our family member? Logic and rationality are lost by extremism.

The Second kind of extremism is done by rulers and politicians. With the ego of power, they become so intolerant that even a small dissent they find incapable to forgive or to think about introspection.

Extremism is harmful for individuals but beneficial to politicians because it makes people incapable to think reasonably and rationally.

A terror organization of Iraq and Syria killed thousands of people and raped their women and made them sex slaves as they were from a minority community. Do you know why? Because some hundreds of years ago their lord was killed by the army of this community. Have you even thought of people who were being killed and what were they thinking? They were thinking what a madness it is.

The same applies to a country. A mosque was demolished. The reason given was that some hundred years ago, a temple was demolished at this place, and so many people died in riots then.

Politicians and rulers are the real beneficiaries of extremism in the society and people are the biggest loser.

Everybody has some power. Every position holder believes in the power given to him. His position matters to him, whether he is a constable or prime minister, whether he is a businessman or an industrialist. How much he remembers or thinks about his power that thinking strengthens his ego and it will reflect in his personality and his decisions. While dealing in daily life the ego of position and power keep ticking in his mind so he often uses it where he should not use it.

Part 3—

Hidden negativities

Most of the negativities are hidden in our sub-conscious mind and it turns out to be apparent in behaviour. I am trying to explain some hidden negativities.

1. Citizens in the lower-class of society think that they need to struggle daily for their survival. They think that their biggest dream is having their own house in their lifetime, they don't think of being millionaires but their aim is to achieve a standard of living like those people for whom they work. Labour class think that the rich class have right to speak rudely to them because they are rich and they accept them. Labour class thinks that the whole system favours the rich and if any crime is committed they should not fight back. This is their hidden negativity and a negative reality.

2. Citizens from the middle-class of society think that they must have their own home, their own car, good education for their children, enough money for old age, etc. But they also believe that they should not be in any conflict with the rich because the system will always favours the rich. This is the hidden negativity in the middle class.

3. Citizens in the upper-class of society think they must become ultra rich. They must leave a great empire for their children and they should do whatever is required for them to achieve this goal. They believe that they can indulge in unjust behaviour and as per circumstances any crime with the labour class and middle-class will not be penalized or punished for that. This is the hidden negativity of upper class.

Acceptance of injustice and being guilty of injustice are both negativities and this negativity transfers from parent to children and is long-lasting.

- Public services in developing countries are dealing and struggling with internal corruption. The reason behind corruption is to achieve the standard of living of successful businessmen. Public servants know that their salary is not enough to fulfil their ambitions. And they don't want to resign also from their job because they think it is too risky so they resort to corruption to fulfil their ambition. When corruption is done, injustice automatically happens because corruption and injustice are complementary to each other. Injustice done to somebody creates negativity in the personality of that public servant and this negativity transfers from him to his children and this is hidden negativity.

- Youth between the age of 16 to 25 get attracted to the film industry. They think that there is glamour, fame, money and it fulfils their youthful aspirations. They think that becoming a renowned artist will be an everlasting adventure and their classmates and friends will never be able to reach their level.

- Most of them try to act in self-made videos, they look in the mirror, and practice hard. They realize that to get there you need looks with physique, or a finest talent in any of the fields of the film industry. But they don't lose courage but everybody in their family and relation make fun of them and reject them. They are ridiculed at every point when such individuals become public servants or employees of any organization they have a feeling that if they have got the contacts, opportunity or platform, they might lead a different life. This feeling becomes a hurdle in their professional growth because they consider their job as trivial where there is no respect, no fame, no money, as compared to the film industry. This is also a kind of hidden negativity.

- I have found that youth aspire for power more than money at an early age. Most of the youth when the hangover of the film Industry is down then they aspire to become a civil servant (in India it is IAS, IPS, IRS, IFS). Aspiration of power is due to the desire to get respect from everybody. Many prepare for the exam to clear prelims and many clear the main exam but as the seats are few, many get selected in another job, than the one they keep preparing for and at last most of them have to satisfy themselves with the designation they get in other public services. They always remain disgruntled that if they had prepared a bit more they would have been selected as a civil servant. Then they feel for many years that their public or private service is trivial and their negativity affects negatively their professional growth. This is a hidden negativity.

- Many employees don't get promotions as fast as their batch mates or their colleagues. They feel they have the same talent and they remain disgruntled in their heart and it affects their professional growth negatively. This is a hidden negativity.

- Many employees remain disgruntled regarding their unfair transfer or posting at the current workplace and it affects their professional growth negatively. This is also a hidden negativity.

- Many public representative senior officers and public in higher-class of society become addicted to respect and honour. When they don't get respect from someone then they feel that their ego is hurt. They think to harm that person or want to ask him why you did not give me respect and many times it happens when people who did not give them respect are the people whom they don't employ or govern but actually they have been appointed to serve them. This is also a hidden negativity when people in power forget their role in society.

- There are some people in society who are lower in class than you, lower in designation and hardly rich but are very close to their principles, and are honest and loving. They deserve respect but many people don't give them respect thinking that giving respect to them publicaly is like disrespecting yourself. This is a wrong notion and a hidden negativity in society.

• If an auto-rickshaw driver, a rickshaw-puller, a carpenter, a labourer, a cobbler are not governed or employed by us then why should we demand respect from these people. If they are honest in their work, we need to respect them. If you give them respect, it must not be told and shown as your kindness, it is your duty.

Known Negativities

Crime, Corruption, inefficiency, injustice are known negativities. Criminal inaction is also part of negativity.

• **Crime**— crime is of two kinds. One is organized crime and the second is unorganized crime. Organized crime can be controlled but unorganized crime cannot be controlled or stopped from occurring. Unorganized crime can be reduced to a minimum level through speedy action and speedy delivery of justice over a period of time. Organized crime is done for financial benefit and it is pre-planned and unorganized crime occurs in anger or ignorance when a person loses his temper during a clash in his family, in his neighborhood or in his relations. He then ignores the consequences of his actions and commits a crime or some person blinded by greed or lust to such extent that he ignores the consequences of his action and crime is committed. Speedy action by police and speedy delivery of justice creates a memory of society that the public is not able to ignore the consequences of the crime which they are thinking to commit. If organized crime is increasing in any state or country then believe me it is supported by state leadership.

• **Corruption**— corruption is the consequence of greed. But it is also the consequence of the criminal inaction of the responsible, and corruption is a joint effort. Corruption may be done by a single person but it cannot be executed successfully without support of more than one person, corruption is an endless chain. Initially, a person is involved in corruption to fulfil his dreams but later he continues to maintain his goodwill and empire. Corruption is a much used short cut to become rich. Being involved in corruption for a longer time makes a person insensitive and sometimes cruel.

Every public servant, politician or businessman has ambitions. People with whom you come in contact, if their standard of living is higher than your and they are in your friends' circle or contact circle then you wish to have the same standard of living. If you are a public servant or a politician then you try to find a way to attain such a standard of living and it forces you to be corrupt. Some people are extremely ambitious since childhood, there are very high chances of such people becoming corrupt. The government organizations must find such candidates in interviews and should prefer to not give them jobs in their organizations.

Corruption is a crime against your own soul. It should not be seen as a crime of a minor nature. Corruption is equal to murders and rapes. If somebody is guilty of corruption for some crore rupees or some hundred crore rupees in a government contract which hardly surfaces ever then he is not just doing a scam with tax-payers' money but he is also complicit in crime occurring in the country. He is also complicit in the deaths occurring due to the lack of healthcare facilities in the country. He is complicit in deaths occurring due to starvation and malnutrition in the country. Because if this money was saved then it could be spent to save the lives in these sectors.

Corruption occurs for so many reasons but these three reasons are important—monetary favours, sexual favours and positional favours. In 90 per cent cases corruption happens for monetary favours, in a very few cases for sexual favours but many cases and mainly in politics and bureaucracy people please their boss with money and sex to gain a higher position. When action taken to accept a monetary favour, it will be called corruption and when action is not taken to stop corruption knowingly will also be called corruption.

- **Inefficiency**— learning skills are essential to work in a higher position. Learning skills demand mental and physical labour. Most people may be ready to do physical labour but due to some mental blocks, negativity or mental lethargy they avoid mental labour and convince themselves that they can survive even without learning these skills for this position or in this position, and hence their inefficiency takes birth. People are working these days in so many posts without having the required skill sets and thus inefficiency enters our bureaucratic and political system. Many of the politicians and bureaucrats are just doing their duty as a caretaker instead of the head of the department. They are not guiding, planning, executing, monitoring and reforming wherever it is most important. People are seen to be satisfied with them.

Expectation of people in developing countries have become so low from the politicians and bureaucrats that if a politician or bureaucrat does 10 to 20 percent better work than the previous person they clap for them because may be earlier they have seen utter incompetency.

Power is sometimes harmful for the efficiency of a politician or public servant. When respected by everybody, such a person keeps thinking about his clout of power, and thinking about several praises he remain in a state of bliss. Then a small dissent or disrespect breaks this bliss and he gets angry. This bliss makes him forget to think about his job. He does not plan, he does not want to see the faults of his working and he is not moved by compassion. And at last he does not remain a down-to-earth person. A person who is not down-to-earth cannot benefit the society or the nation even if he holds all the power and money of the planet. Compassion in your heart should always be more important than the bliss in your mind, because only then you can benefit the society or the nation.

- **Injustice—** everything which is not justice to someone is injustice. There are so many forms of injustices in the world but the first injustice while doing injustice with somebody is an injustice with your soul and an injustice with your soul is an injustice to god. It means if you do injustice with anybody then you are doing injustice to god, and people who do injustice to god don't have the right to pray in any temple, mosque, gurudwara, or church. When the soul of a person is hurt, he cannot attain mental peace. Every injustice done to your soul or god will come to you in such a proportion that you will not be able to handle the situation.

Corruption is a form of injustice. When somebody takes money for doing their job from a poor person like providing a government service for which he is being paid already by the government and taking money is not allowed then he is doing injustice. He is taking a part of the income or saving of that poor person which he could use for his personal necessities. He may not be punished by the government but his soul surely will punish him.

People taking money illegally for providing any government service or issue order in their favour or against somebody or diluting the law in their hands are doing injustice to the people for whom to serve that they were appointed.

People who are implementing the morally wrong orders of the government or anybody to stay in their office or to continue to receive benefit they are receiving are doing Injustice not only to those people but to god.

If we see history, we will find many nations who saw severe downfall because at some period of time their rulers did injustice to some people or so many people. The entire population of the country had to suffer because they were complicit in this crime because they voted that ruler into power and they did not oppose the ruler when injustice was being done. So, it was the turn of God to do justice.

When the collective conscience of the nation or the world or the specific area feel depressed due to the injustices done by men then natural disasters occur.

So many injustices done by men in his daily routine and one of those is eating non-veg, eating of non-veg is a severe crime in the eyes of God. Killing animals is a crime because they are being killed to feed you.

Crime is also a form of injustice, when crime is committed in anger, greed or lust then it is an injustice with the victim. That is why police and courts have been set up to provide justice. Injustice being done because of crime are less in nature than injustice being done because of corruption.

Corruption, crime and injustice are related with one another in such a way that they cannot be parted. Crime is injustice and injustice is a crime and both cannot exist without corruption.

The main reason for prevalent crime, corruption and injustice in the society is that public servants and politicians say that they have been appointed to serve the people but inside they strongly feel that they are owners of the people. With the struggle of so many years, they have reached this position, so they feel themselves as a ruler instead of a servant, and this is the fault of democracy.

A dictator will never feel himself as a servant and a servant will never feel himself as a dictator.

This is also right that a politician may have to take such decisions sometimes which is against public opinion but beneficial for the nation. But it is also right that these kind of decisions consist only 10 per cent of overall decisions.

There is unlimited kind of justices such as injustices done by an employer to an employee. injustice done by wife to husband and children to their old age parents. Though every injustice can't be explained but it is negative nonetheless.

How to Kill Negativity

We have to see that what is the age and depth of negativity in someone's mind. Then we need to have a proper counselling of that person until negativity is not removed from his mind. Motivation will not work without counselling. For example, if we don't start a car's engines with the key of counselling then the accelerator of motivation will not move the car.

As far as the question of negativities in employees, we need to remove the reason of negativity from the mind of the employee with counselling and once he starts believing that he can complete the task then the accelerator of motivation can be given at intervals. If a psychiatrist can heal the mind and cure deadly mental disorders with counselling and motivation then we can put our employees on the path of progress with counselling and motivation.

Way of Counselling

- If a youngster is negative about marriage, counsel him him telling him the various statistics and facts about marriage, which shows him the positive outcomes of marriage. Tell him about the requirement of old age and importance of a life partner. Tell him how married life enhances the personal and professional growth of a person. Show him videos and give him examples of people who are living joyfully after so many years of marriage.

- If an employee is negative about a task or work, show him the video of the highest performers of that task, and show him how he managed to achieve such a big target. Teach him the mechanism, listen to his point of view, understand his mindset and his circumstances. Visit his office once and stay there for a whole day and observe his working style and then counsel him for the better. Once he get started, push him forward with the motivation.

- If someone is negative about the country, then we should ask him what are the things he does not like about his country? We need to tell him about the social and economic situation of the country—when the country got freedom and about the current scenario. He may be comparing his country with developed nations. Instead we need to tell him the condition of under developed countries. It may be right that his country and its system has so many deficiencies but we need to ask him what he is doing to improve this? If he has voted judiciously in the last election, is he supporting so many people trying to win an election who are honest and efficient? Is he contributing in increasing awareness in the society about what is being done and what can be and should be done in his country? If he is not doing these things then he does not have the right to be negative about his country.

- If somebody is negative about politics in the country or the world then he needs to introspect. Bad politics is an outcome of badly informed decisions of voters. If somebody is taking advantage of you, it is not his fault, it is your fault. It is right that in the last 70 years the quality of leadership is in decline continuously while the education level in all these countries kept improving. It is due to religious and caste system based polarization of educated fools. Today's politics is the politics of comfort and glamour. It is right that it is all negative but being negative will not improve anything, we need to work hard to improve it.

- If somebody is negative about a particular religion then we should try to know the reason behind it. We need to tell them every religion in this world is not in the format when it was written or propagated. And this is due to the further unauthorized changes by religious leaders in the holy books, customs, etc. When religion was propagated, it was the finest for that group of population.

Inaction

Inaction means to not do something which is expected from you as per your role, designation, your family, your personal or professional life. Inaction is of four kinds:

1. Inaction due to laziness
2. Inction due to negativity
3. Inaction due to addiction
4. Inaction seeing benefit in mind

1. **Inaction due to laziness** – When somebody knows that he needs to do something in order to achieve their personal and professional goals but they don't do so due to laziness or they don't want to come out of their comfort zone, it is called inaction due to laziness. Inaction due to laziness is a major reason for loss of productivity of a person.

    See example—Rahul was very active in his personal or professional life but for some years he has become so lethargic. He wakes up in the morning, has bed tea, a bath and comes to office and here he does what is mandatory and does not make an effort to achieve the goals given to him. He always remains in his comfort zone and does not like to do anything which is out of his daily routine. It is called inaction due to laziness.

2. **Inaction due to negativity**— Many people don't act thinking that it is too difficult for them or it will not be morally right or they will not be able to complete the task or the task given to them is impractical, and it is called inaction due to negativity.

    See example—Umesh is an active person. He wakes up early in the morning. Has a good run, baths and comes to office. He has been assigned a task by his boss but he thinks he will not be able to complete the task so he does not even start the task. He can also think that completing the task will put him in trouble in the long run or the task is not ethically right.

It is called inaction due to negativity which means fear, anxiety, and thinking that I can't do this or I will not be successful in doing this.

3. **Inaction due to addiction**—people who are addicted to alcohol, smoking or chewing tobacco feel that they can't complete the task if they feel that they can but their addiction does not let them. Addiction acquires a big space in your mind and a lot of time is wasted in feeling its requirement, consuming it and feeling the bliss after having consumed the addicted product.

See example—Ramesh was an addict of alcohol. He was given a task by his boss but before performing the task, he consumed alcohol and suddenly he felt that he is unable to finish the routine work of his job. He forgets about the task and leaves the office.

There is another kind of addiction and that is addiction of social media and speading time talking with your loved ones. These addictions also play a significant role in less productivity of employees.

Inaction means I want to do it but I don't do it. Second I need to do it but I don't want to do it.

A manager needs to plan a task and he constantly think about the task but if he invests his free time in checking social media or talking to loved ones then firstly he will not get enough time to think about the task and secondly his mind will get diverted from the task.

4. **Inaction seeing benefit**- This kind of in action is when a person sees that action will not benefit but inaction in the specific task will give more benefit.

Different Kinds of Inactions and Its Costs

There are unlimited kinds of inactions out of which I am trying to explain a few. Inaction has its cost for the person, organization, nation or the world but it firstly recover its cost from the person who is suffering from it.

1. If an employee does not perform his duties diligently, he may lose his job or if he is in government service he may lose his next promotion.

2. If a politician remains inactive or becomes inactive in his constituency or in the work area, if he stops caring for the people, if he does not do what is expected from him then he may lose an election for another term.

3. If police remain inactive in a law and order situation, it may cause several causalities and injuries to the general public, and in its consequence, policemen may get suspension.

4. Judicial inaction can lead a country into chaos. If the judiciary does not do what is right and becomes inactive then the whole nation can run into chaos.

5. If the head of a business becomes inactive then his business may fail and cost him huge losses.

6. If the army of a nation becomes inactive then the whole nation can become a slave of another country.

7. If a head of a nation or state becomes inactive then there are so many chances for that country to turn into chaos.

8. If parents become inactive then upbringing of their children may be faulty and there may be so many negative consequences for such parents.

The whole world is running due to action and the whole world will suffer due to inaction.

Distraction of Thoughts

One of the main reasons of non-performance is distraction of thoughts. When a person decides to do something like study or completing a task, then controlling the thoughts and stopping distractions is a big challenge. Difference between a successful person and an unsuccessful person is their concentration power.

See example—a student sitting in the room thinking that he will complete this chapter in one sitting. But his mind is somewhere else. He sits forcefully focused on the book after ten minutes he got a random thought and then another thought related with the previous and then suddenly comes a thought which is related with the work this student enjoys doing. And then this student starts thinking about that work and stops studying.

Many times, lack of concentration is the outcome of disliking the work which is mandatory for us. People in any job whether it is public or private think that they don't like their job. They think that they are doing this job just for a livelihood but they don't enjoy their job. Many people don't have any specific hobby or any interest where they can find an alternative to earn to their livelihood. Whatever the results of companies, whether public or private, are the outcome of the efforts who are not working wholeheartedly. Everyone is doing what is mandatory for them to survice.

Many people, especially most of the young people are addicted to social media. A clock is keep ticking in their mind to check social media (if anybody posted anything useful for them).

They enjoy themselves and in their free time they firstly check the social media.

Many employees are used to talking to their family members and friends so much that whenever they get free time they start talking to them.

Whatever obsession a person has, his thoughts will keep making an effort to get close to that obsession. People who have addiction of any kind, then their addiction becomes their obsession and need. And their thoughts make an effort to draw close to their these obsessions.

The human mind always keeps thinking about something. It thinks about what it enjoys. Most of the time Human thinks thoughts about sensation, reward or highly negative aspects like losses or fears. But humans tend to move towards these thoughts only when a stimulus is given to them. Otherwise, most of the time humans think about subjects of comfort zone. The human mind tends to move avoid subjects which it does not like or enjoy, or those which demands greater mental labour. Likeable thoughts become habit and soon habit becomes an obsession as in the cases of fears and losses.

Different Kind of Distractions

A child while trying to concentrate on study suddenly has a thought related to watching TV cartoons and he gets distracted.

A child of thirteen, concentrating on studying suddenly get a thought of playing cricket outdoors and get distracted.

A boy of 18 years, concentrating on studying suddenly get a thought of his crush and gets distracted.

A boy at the age of 23, preparing for competitive exams suddenly get a thought of checking social media and get distracted.

Distractions or obsession of social media is found in all age groups. Employees of a company or a firm also got distracted by social media, talking to loved ones, etc. After becoming a parent, a parent may also be distracted from his work due to his care for his childrens.

A man is inclined to think about the hot topic of national or regional media. A human finds himself unable to control his obsession.

Some common social media distractions are:

• Let me see, what these persons have written?

• Let me check, these people write at this time every day?

• Let me see, who has liked or commented on my post?

• Let me see, who is online?

- Let me see, what is happening in the world?
- Let me see, if he/she has posted a new profile picture or something else?

How to Avoid Distractions

Distraction can be avoided by self-discipline or by a sense of urgency or compulsions.

Through self-discipline: Self-discipline can be achieved by self-awareness. You must determine a point of thought and your thoughts must not wander from it. As soon as your thoughts wander from it, you must again bring your focus to that thought. After practicing for several days, you will find that you have become capable to concentrate well.

Through urgency or compulsions: When a compulsion or urgency gets attached to a task, everybody strives for it irrespective if they get or not. You have seen that when you are on leave, you avoid a bath or early waking up because on holiday it is not mandatory. So, if you think about it deeply that you have to do this work compulsorily then you will surely do it whether you get success or not.

When you study, think that tomorrow is your exam then you will feel a compulsion that you have to do your best to study. It is same as when you have to complete some work and it solely depends on you, think that tomorrow I have to present it to my seniors so I need to finish it today.

Procrastination

If a person procrastinates his work even if he has enough time and chance to complete his work then it is called procrastination.

Procrastination is a result of the decisions taken by the sub-conscious mind. Decisions taken by the sub-conscious mind are the compulsions of obsessions habits and the products of the comfort zone. Most of the time these decisions are more powerful than the decision of the conscious mind. There is a relationship of boss and employee between the sub-conscious mind and conscious mind. Most of the time a decision is already taken and the conscious mind is forced to implement it. If somebody has decided to check social media or someone has decided to drink or smoke then the decision is already taken. The conscious mind just has to implement it.

The real work of counselling and motivation is to empower the conscious mind so much that it will reject the orders of the sub-conscious mind and refuse to implement it.

Procrastination results in non-completion of work. How an employee delays some work in the evening thinking that he will do it tomorrow. And tomorrow he thinks that I will do it the next day and soon when this work becomes a mammoth size that same employee finds himself in trouble. Often that employee throws that work into the dustbin or ask his seniors for help.

Most of the time reason for procrastination is one's comfort zone. People have made their habits and they don't want to leave them. For example, spending most of their time on smartphone, alcohol, smoking or chewing tobacco or leaving office at a certain time, it all happens sub-consciously.

Procrastination is a habit that a person with comfort zone develops over a period of time related to his personal and professional work thinking that it is not necessary to finish this work today.

There are two circumstances—one is when you don't get the time during the whole day to finish that work then it will not be called procrastination and second, when you have time but you take a decision to not finish it today.

Different Kinds of Procrastination

There are many kinds of procrastination—one is that kind of procrastination that this work requires greater mental labour or it is too tough to do. Second is that it is easy to do and I can do it anytime so I am procrastinating it. Third is the procrastination due to distractions. When a person is going to do the work and he is mentally ready to do that work. he suddenly gets distracts by social media or any other subject of comfort zone. This consumes so much of his time and energy that he does not find time to do much work in the evening. Hence, the work is already procrastinated. Fourth is the procrastination due to self-satisfaction. When you have done a lot of work in a day and have achieved so many targets that you feel self-satisfaction, then you believe that this work can be done tomorrow.

How to Avoid Procrastination

Procrastination can be avoided only by time management. You must know how much time you have and how much work you have to finish. So, if work is more and time is less then select the most important work first and finish it. Second, kill your time killers like social media. Its use should be restricted during office hours or if necessary then only it should be allowed for a few minutes. Your other obsessions and compulsions time must be limited for a few minutes only. Many times, if you have to sit for half an hour or an hour more to finish the work then do so. Pending work is damaging for your career and image.

If procrastination has to be avoided then people need to come out of their comfort zones. There are two ways to bring people out of their comfort zones. First is reward and second is punishment. Punishment creates negativity, it does not only harm that person but also harms the organization in the long-term. This is also true that rewards cannot be given to everybody but through counselling and motivation we can transform a person. Money is a great motivation in itself.

When we punish people for not coming out of their comfort zone, they panic and complete the work but again they go into their comfort zone and after some time they become shameless.

The best way to deal with such people is by giving them smaller targets according to their capabilities. When they achieve their targets, honour and reward them, and make them feel valuable. Every month increase their target by 10 to 20 per cent, and within one year you will find that the employee is achieving as much which cannot be imagined before one year by this employee.

Indiscipline

To understand indiscipline, we need to understand discipline. The word discipline has all the answers of life's problems. Discipline means you do what you expect from yourself in your personal and professional life. Discipline means one has control over his mind and body. Approximately more than 90 per cent of the world's population is not disciplined. The main impediment in achieving a disciplined life is one's addiction and diversion of thoughts. Indiscipline has many reasons: negativity, inaction, distractions and ultimately lack of self-control.

Indiscipline is when your employee comes late on a regular basis and when you ask, object or discuss it with him he shows ego. Indiscipline is when an employee does not comply with the instructions of his boss and also when he speaks rudely to his boss.

But there is also one more aspect that we need to discuss. Sometimes, what a boss thinks as discipline the employee thinks as exploitation.

The second aspect is when the boss is scolding his employee to such an extent that the employee loses his temper and speaks rudely his boss.

From the point of view of your boss, if you fulfil what is expected of you in your job then you are disciplined. From the point of view of your family, if you fulfil what is expected of you it then you are disciplined. But in my point of view if your mind and body are in your control then you are disciplined.

If you can't control your mind then you are not a disciplined person. If you have any addiction then you can't control your mind. The only way to control your mind is to think less. Do things without thinking too much. People who thinks too much can't control their minds.

Roots of Indiscipline

Indiscipline is not found in employees who have become financially independent. If they are annoyed with their bosses, they think if they lost their job, they will not have to face financial turmoil.

Indiscipline is found in employees who don't like the job but are doing it for financial reasons.

One day they become so frustrated and it reflects in their behaviour. Sometimes an employee is so sad or annoyed due to any reason in his personal life that it reflects as indiscipline in his behaviour at office.

As far as the question of non-punctuality and less effort are the indiscipline happen due to comfort zone that we have discussed in the previous chapters.

Different kinds of indiscipline

Personal Indiscipline – when a person does not take care of his body and his family, then it is personal indiscipline.

Professional indiscipline—when a person does not take care of his professional responsibilities, it is called professional indiscipline. E.g.: non-punctuality, hot talks with juniors and seniors, etc.

Social indiscipline—when a person does not behave like a responsible citizen in the society, it is called social indiscipline such as making neighbours uncomfortable with noise, fighting with people over petty issues, etc.

Relationship of Creativity with Indiscipline

A more disciplined person is always less creative because a disciplined person is capable to control his thought and when thoughts are controlled creativity cannot enter in one's mind. That is why, it has been found that people who are more creative such as writers scientists, artists, etc. are less disciplined.

Political leaders can become ministers but they can't make best policies until they are creative. A leader needs to be more creative than disciplined. A businessman also requires creativity to expand and modify his business. A more disciplined and less creative leader cannot be successful on real terms.

As far as the question arises of service-class, then people in lower positions require more discipline and less creativity but as they are promoted to higher positions they need to be more creative.

Creativity is about finding a solution to a problem and discipline is required to implement that solution.

A person who can control his thoughts can wake up early, do workout, and report to his job on time. He can also perform better with hard work but is unable to do any creative work.

There is a truth if you see. In the whole world people who believe in their physical capabilities hardly believe in their mental capabilities and people who believe in their mental capabilities hardly believe in their physical capabilities. There are very few exception to this rule either that person is a saint or a fool.

Focus, Priorities and Multitasking

Everyone has a personal and professional life. Sometimes an employee thinks about the priorities of office while at home and sometimes the employee does not decide beforehand. He reaches office and then determine the priorities. While at work in office the employee is determined to do so many things but after reaching home, his focus turned towards his family life. When he comes to office next day he takes some time to get that focus back.

When an individual reaches office he takes a look at work and decides priorities but priorities keep changing due to multitasking and by the evening he finds that tasks by multitasking are completed but what he decided to do in the morning has been not started yet.

There are many kinds of priorities

1. **Daily priorities**—Every individual has to fulfil his responsibilities. There are some responsibilities which are of a daily nature like family responsibilities, coming to office and office work, etc. Up to a certain age till children are not grown up, the focus of the individuals remains at first on their family responsibilities.

2. **Monthly priorities**—At monthly intervals individuals have to pay their bills and EMIS, and have to do shopping for their family needs. Targets for the month are also allotted at monthly intervals to individuals .Self-aware people keep on tracking their progress on a daily basis and keep making an effort.

3. **Long-term priorities**—These kinds of priorities are related to an individual's career, promotions, business, house, car, status, annual targets, education of children, etc.

The human mind is prone to think about long-term goals and the pleasure of achieving these goals which creates a hindrance in the efforts that needs to be made to accomplish these goals.

Priorities of the conscious mind are always right as demanded by your job or business. But priorities of the sub-conscious mind rule your day like addiction or subjects of one's comfort zone.

The Managerial Mindset

There are so many roles a manager plays in different aspects of life.

Manager as a counsellor—The main motive of counselling in business is to sell its products or services. As a business head you often need to counsel your employees at various stages to make them self-aware. Counselling is a two-way process, you need to put forth your view and also you need to listen to the other person and then you need to satisfy them with your argument.

While in service, it means if you are in the public sector or private sector as a manager, you will need to counsel your employees and your customers. Before counselling your employees you need to experience their working style. You must know what is the mental state of your employee, then you need to make them self-aware. Once they realize their faults, then you need to motivate them.

Manager as a counsellor in the family—A person with a managerial mindset needs to counsel his family members on different occasions. Sometimes he needs to counsel his wife, his children, and sometimes his siblings and parents. When a person counsels, he must be prepared to change his view. If arguments of the other person are valid then you need to change also. A person in a managerial position can resolve all conflicts in his family.

Society also needs counselling. Here, society means relatives, neighbours and friends. A person who counsels better will have cordial relations with the society.

If a political leaders has a managerial mindset then he may be aware of the public grievances. As he thinks to persuade people over an issue he can do it with counselling.

Manager as a motivator—In a business, the head of a business often needs to motivate his employees through words and actions. In services, a manager needs to motivate his employees regularly through words, action and rewards. Both in business and services, come ups and downs and in the time of upheaval motivation becomes too important and when there is no situation of crisis the motivation is required to improve the performances.

The same applies to the family, in the time of crisis or in a normal situation children need motivation.

Same as in a society when there are riots and epidemics in the society or in the nation then a person with a managerial mindset needs to counsel and motivate the society.

Manager as an administrator—Administration is required in all spheres of life. In business and services, you often need to apply it over the employees whose wrong habits have become so strong that counselling and motivation do not work on them.

Sometimes a person with a managerial mindset needs to apply administration over the family members. For example, children who are going on a wrong path, counselling and motivation don't work on them.

Administration is sometimes required in politics too. When officers under your control don't perform and it harms public interest then you need to administer them. Sometimes when people become so aggressive that they harm public property or public lives then it is required for a politician to apply administration over them.

Manager as a leader—Firstly let us know what leadership is. When a person often shows that he can do a work and over a period of time he has shown it. And his colleagues, juniors and seniors have confidence in him and he also believes that he can finish the task, then he is a leader. Example of a leadership is when people come to follow you and have faith in your abilities to lead without any personal interest or benefit. It has been seen that managers who have sufficient leadership qualities are the ones for whom employees work more without demanding any monetary benefit. In business, a business head with leadership quality and managerial aptitude can reach greater heights. In services, a manager needs to have leadership qualities. Often when a task is given to him, firstly he needs to guide his team on how the task should be performed. A manager always needs to lead from the front during a task or a crisis.

In the family, a person with a managerial mindset always leads from the front and takes care of all the needs of his family.

He takes care of his family, counsels them, motivates them, administers them and leads them from the front in joys and in sorrows.

In society, a person with a managerial mindset always leads for the good cause and leaders are made. Managerial qualities are not inherited in leaders but leadership qualities are inherited in managers.

Manager as a problem solver—There are always problems and challenges arising daily in the business. A business head needs to be a problem-solver so that business can run smoothly.

In services, a manager needs to have a problem-solving attitude. So many problems related to HR, operations, marketing, etc arise and a manager needs to find a solution for it.

A problem-solving person is required everywhere whether it is business, job, society, family or politics. This ability is required less in family but to a great extent in society, job and politics.

Manager as a manager—A manager's most important skill is management. Counselling, motivation, administration, leadership and problem-solving skills are called management as a whole. If someone has these skills then he is a good manager. Now the question is how to develop these skills in someone.

1. **How to develop counselling skill**—First virtue required is patience to listen to the other person. The second virtue required is to observe silently. Third virtue required is analytical ability and fourth virtue is having a basic knowledge of psychology and having fondness for collecting experiences. These virtues will develop a different level of communication skill in that person and he will be able to counsel better.

2. **Motivation**—A managers needs to know the mental state of his employee and as per circumstances, he needs to motivate his employees on a day-to-day basis. It is necessary for a manager to believe in motivation. With a story sometimes is

more beneficial. Motivation through appreciation is always better.

3. **Administration**—Administration is required when counselling and motivation do not work or the employee does not take it seriously. While administering, a manager needs to have his mind closed. An administrator needs to give his dose of administration in such a quantity that the employee won't go into depression and his urgency and compulsion thermometers are awakened. To administer, we need to behave like a strong person.

4. **Leadership**—Leadership is the outcome of self-confidence and experience of application of self-confidence and succeeding. As far as the question of leadership, over confidence is never a bad thing. Self-confidence when added to desire gives birth to enthusiasm and enthusiasm is the first ingredient of a successful life. Enthusiasm is a positive emotion and is required to complete any task. Now, the question is how to create self-confidence in someone who is hopeless? Through counselling we need to persuade him to have an artificial belief in himself that he can complete the task. With guidance and support get the task done. It will create an original self-confidence in that person again. Give him an achievable task and he will get it done. You will find that this person is now full of self-confidence. Now you can give him a leadership role.

5. **Problem-solving skill**—Real life problem is very different than theoretical maths or reasoning problem-solving. Every person who has a problem, solves it within the ambit of his knowledge and experiences. Problem persists when you don't acknowledge a problem as a problem or when you believe that this problem cannot be solved. To have a great capacity to solve the problem, your knowledge and experience must be wide. For innovation or to solve a problem, you must have a resolve that I have to think, and I have to devise an idea that nobody has ever thought of.

Problem can be solved in two ways, first is through learning and experience and second through innovations. It depends on the extent of the problem that how fast it can be solved. To solve a problem-one needs to know about the origin of the problem and its causes. To have a solution for a problem, one needs to believe deeply that this problem is nothing for him and he can solve it easily. When a problem appears in front of a person, he knows that he has adequate knowledge or experience to solve this problem or not. If he thinks he does not have adequate nowledge and experience then firstly needs he to gain these from people, books and internet.

Problem-solving is the most important skill a person needs to become successful. Suppose, there are two person. One has all the knowledge and experience but he lacks self-confidence and second is person who has enormous self-confidence but lacks knowledge and experience. Chances are thate the problem will be solved by the second person. Because knowledge and experience can be gained through self-confidence but the person who lacks self-confidence will not even try to solve the problem. There are experts in every field but their self-confidence and creativity is not sufficient and most people in senior positions depend on experts to solve a problem.

Sometimes, the solution is so simple that nobody thinks of it. Problem-solving demands devotion and full focus in searching for a solution. When there is a solution, it is most of the time not accurate but through modification it could become accurate.

Questions and Answers

Q- Can you explain and suggest the solution for the negativity before and after marriage?

Ans- Film industry and porn industry have raised the sexual aspiration of individuals very high. Men and women aspire to have their life-partner looking like some actor and actresses. Males think that their wife should be fair, tall, etc. and women think that their partner should be tall, smart looking with good stamina but they don't get what they want because marriage is not just about sex. It is a relationship between husband and wife and their families. Parents consider everything for the better future of their child.

When love happens, an individual gives less importance to sex but when there is an arranged marriage, an individual always thinks about the looks of his/her partner. Every human being does not get his or her ideal partner according to one's expectations. Anyone of the two or both may feel that their sexual satisfaction level is low but they console themselves and this negativity exists for years. When one finds a chance or opportunity to fulfil his or her repressed sexual desires then they go onto the wrong path and relationships are broken.

Materialistic minds are more prone to this but spiritual minds also sometimes become victim of this trait.

Love is the antidote of negativity in a marital relationship. Where love is strong, every negativity remains subdued and the relationship prospers but if the content of love in a relationship goes lower than negativity then the relationship breaks.

In a relationship where expectations are very high and love is low, there are more chances that the relationship will not continue for a longer period.

Where love is strong, there expectations are less. It is true regarding marriages but it also depends on the mindset of an individual. Where love is stronger, non-fulfilment of expectation does not create stress in a relationship. That is why, it is said that marriages are very fragile for one or two years as after this period it does not let anything or anybody break the relationship.

Q- How do we deal with post-marital conflicts?

Ans- Let us understand with an example of a very beautiful girl and a not so smart boy who fall in love with each other. They both got approval of their families after so much effort and get married. The first month passes beautifully. Suddenly the girl felt that she want to live separately with her husband as she does not like the family of the boy. When the boy comes home from the job in the evening, she expresses her thoughts. The boy could not agree with her as he loves his family and he thought that it will be an insult to his family.

The girl made an issue and said that she was going to her mother's house. The girl was right in her perspective and the boy was right in his perspective. They both did not had a proper dialogue and now their relationship is on the brink of an end. Sometimes being right does not solve the problem. So, there was a need to apply managerial mindset by the boy. If the lady was adamant, the man was suppose to ask for some months time and in this period they need to strengthen their bond. If the bond is strengthened then they can both adjust to some extent and the relationship will go on.

Q- What was different in developed countries compared to under-developed or developing countries?

Ans- In many of the developing and under-developed countries, one thing is common and that is gender bias. So many restrictions on women have made these countries poorly educated. If we see the history of the last 50 years of these countries and developed countries we shall find that in under-developed and developing countries, education, healthcare, corruption, justice was never an election issue, whereas in the developed countries education, healthcare, corruption and justice were always the election issues. As education was never an election issue. So political leaders did not work on it. The lack of proper education, religion, sect, caste ruled the election and public gets what they voted for. These countries and its citizens remain poor. Most of them become victims of corruption and injustice. But in Western countries, there was no such gender bias since there are educated citizens. Citizens made real issues of corruption, employment, education, health, justice, etc. as the primary issues of election.

Leaders got elected over these issues and they worked on these issues. These nations grew exponentially and became developed nations.

Q – Is it right to have mercy for oneself?

Ans- Don't have mercy for yourself. It leads to laziness, overeating, crime, corruption and it is the biggest reason of inaction.

See the example—if a person is obese, seeing the burger he would think that he has been advised by the doctor to not eat junk food. Then he will have mercy over himself and that feeling of mercy says to him that sometimes you can eat, it will do no harm and he eats the burger. Same as diabetics, seeing a sweet dish, mercy activitates and, he thinks that I have not eaten sweet dishes a for long time why not give it a chance. Same for a rapist, seeing a woman he thinks to rape her, he knows that it is a moral and legal crime but the mercy activates and it says to him that nobody would get to know, so he moves forward. When a person asks for a bribe, he knows that he is wrong but he has enormous mercy over himself and that made him think that everybody is taking a bribe, it is a normal thing. If a customer is paying me a bribe, so what? I am doing this work for him. My friends are moving in luxury cars, is it not my duty to achieve that status of living? Is it not my duty to take care of my family well?

Q- What is the reason behind hatred getting spread and believed in the world?

Ans- Behind all hatreds, there is politics. Hatred benefits politics, so they spread it.

See an example—Here, no issues of Shia-Sunni conflicts is seen in India even though the Muslim population of India is more than their population in Pakistan. In Pakistan and other Islamic countries, there is a division between Shias and Sunnis and it appears in media regularly. What is the mystery? Mystery is in India political parties don't see Muslims as Shias and Sunni votebanks. While in Islamic countries, they see them as Shias and Sunnis and then publicize it in the whole nation. The issue of Hindu-Muslim is seen to be same.

Q- Which policy is better for a nation: appeasement of minorities or radicalization of majority?

Ans- Both are condemnable. Both must be prohibited in any nation. Appeasement or radicalization are both done by politics with the support of media and religious leaders.

See example—In Indonesia and Pakistan, Muslims are in majority and while Pakistan is radicalized too much but Indonesia is not. This is because of the politics these countries followed. As far as the question of profit and loss, appeasement is less harmful than radicalization because in appeasement the majority is not shown as an enemy. But in radicalization, the minority is shown as an enemy. But appeasement and acceptance of that appeasement creates pathways for radicalization of majority. Countries who did appeasement of minorities have not harmed itself as much in the history as countries who followed the path of radicalization of majority. Behind appeasement and radicalization, there is no moral force or obligation of political parties or leader, but a desire to capture the votebank. Appeasement and radicalization must be banned in any democracy. Radicalization can never be an answer to appeasement. Discrepancy of governance happens when a government or a political party or leader seems to favour a particular religion, caste or race while neglecting the others. Solution of radicalization is not de-radicalization camps but dialogue and speeches which are correct and equitable in nature by those who are the role models of the society.

Q- What do you think about religion?

Ans- God invented human life and he found that human beings do not live as per rules and regulation of humanity. So, God decided to invent religion. God found that all the world's population could not be covered under one religion so he invented three or four major religions through his sons. The motive of all religions was never to fight with another religion or to finish them. It is only the motive of politicians but its motive is to live under certain rules and to reach God.

Q- What do you think about non-vegetarianism?

Ans- God never wants a human being to kill an animal for food but when these religions were invented, agriculture in the world was not so developed and most of the population of the world had no option but to rely on meat. So God allowed non-vegetarianism in these religions. But now it must be understood that killing an animal is also a kind of violence except in very challenging circumstances. So now humans must give up non-vegetarianism except people who cannot survive without non-veg as per climatic or medical requirements.

Q- What do you think about the caste system of India?

Ans- Caste system in India is the results of "varna vyavastha" of ancient India. Saints of India created "varna vyavastha" when varna was certain as per the profession of individuals. People who used to worship, profess, teach or guide the kingdom were called 'Brahmin', people who used to fight for the kingdom were called 'Kshatriya', people who were in business were called 'Vaishya' and people who used to clean dirty places were called 'Shudra'. That system continued for hundreds of years. Varna vyavastha was linked with profession but later it converted in to identity of these individuals and their generation and it became the caste system of India. Later, so many people changed their profession from cleaning to professing or from business to fighting for the nation. But their caste was not changed and people continue to treat them with disrespect and society of India could not understand this simple truth.

It is same for untouchability. This concept too grew in India, in ancient times. People who used to clean dirty place even after having a bath they smell badly as there was no soap or detergent available at that time. So policy makers profess to everybody to not touch these people and that untouchatility continues even in the present when a very few percentage of people are employed in cleaning activities and most of them get employment somewhere else. People who are employed in cleaning activities now can have a good bath. They smell good but society is unable to understand this simple truth.

The same problem is when a woman menstruates, they are not allowed in the kitchen. It is also the concept of that time when soap, detergent and sanitary pads were not available so they used to smell bad. But now soap, detergents and sanitary pads are available but even then this custom continues in society.

People are classified two kinds, liberals and conservatives. Conservatives can be of two kinds—narrow-minded and broad-minded. It is my experience that with age, education, and wealth, most of the narrow-minded people can turn into broad-minded and also many of them can become liberals. Nations where there is poverty and unemployment are the most backward, dogmatic, bigots and religiously fanatic. An unemployed person spends most of his time seeing television, gossiping and worshipping, consequently it makes him a tool of political and religious fanaticism. When he gets employment and progress, his focus changes to self-progress and he does not have enough time and energy to spend somewhere else. In developing countries, most of the children are brought up by less educated parents and in economically and socially suffocating environment. If they don't get a job early and continue to struggle for survival, there are many chances that they will not turn to a liberal mindset even at the age of 50 or 60.

Corruption is the biggest problem of the world, and poor nations are struggling with the problem of resources. Whatever they spend on education is normally spoilt in corruption. If education is promoted with internal or external help, social evils may be removed from the society even though there can be exceptions.

❏

Ingram Content Group UK Ltd.
Milton Keynes UK
UKHW010643250523
422339UK00004B/127